THE ART OF

MEDITATION

Except the Lord build the house, they
labour in vain that build it.

—Psalm 127

Illumination dissolves all material ties and binds men
together with the golden chains of spiritual understanding; it acknowledges only the leadership of the
Christ; it has no ritual or rule but the divine, impersonal
universal Love; no other worship than the inner Flame
that is ever lit at the shrine of Spirit. This union is the
free state of spiritual brotherhood. The only restraint is
the discipline of Soul, therefore we know liberty without
license; we are a united universe without physical limits;
a divine service to God without ceremony or creed. The
illumined walk without fear—by Grace.

—THE INFINITE WAY

THE ART OF
MEDITATION

JOEL S. GOLDSMITH

HarperSanFrancisco
A Division of HarperCollins*Publishers*

OTHER BOOKS BY JOEL S. GOLDSMITH

The Thunder of Silence

Practicing the Presence

The Art of Spiritual Healing

The Mystical I

Living the Infinite Way

A Parenthesis in Eternity

Our Spiritual Resources

Joel Goldsmith's Gift of Love

FIRST HARPER & ROW PAPERBACK EDITION PUBLISHED IN 1990.

LIBRARY OF CONGRESS CATALOG CARD NUMBER: 56-13258
ISBN: 0-06-250379-0

96   97   RRD H 12   11   10   9

CONTENTS

v

PART THREE

MEDITATION: THE FRUITS

PART ONE

MEDITATION:
THE PRACTICE

CHAPTER I

THE WAY

Most men and women are convinced that there is a divine Power of some sort operating in human affairs; but they are not sure what it is, nor do they know how to bring this divine Presence and Power into their daily experience. There was a time when many of these people were content to believe in a God dwelling in a remote heaven, a God whom they would not meet until after death. In this practical age, however, very few are satisfied with that limited concept of God.

The world is full of discord. The question is asked again and again: Why, if there is a God, does this God permit sin, disease, war, famine, and disaster? How can all these evils be, if God is good, if God is life, if God is love? How can there be that kind of a God *and* the horrors of human experience? People throughout all time have attempted to solve this riddle, but there is no solution; there is no answer except that the world has not known God. We can never for a moment believe that if people in this world had a realization of God, they would have discord and inharmony, too. Discord and inharmony come into our life because of our ignorance of God. As we acquaint now ourselves with Him, we find the secret of harmonious existence.

People throughout all time have sought freedom, peace, and plenty; but their search has been primarily through the feverish activity of the human mind. Pleasure and satisfaction have been artificially created, and because of their artificiality, they are neither permanent nor real. Living out from the level of the mind, there must be a continuous round of new pleasures, new faces, and new scenes. There is rarely a truly joyous moment, nor are there periods of rest and relaxation.

Freedom, peace, and plenty are not dependent upon circumstances or conditions. Men have been free in chains; they have been free under slavery and oppression; they have found peace in the midst of war; they have survived floods and famine; they have prospered in periods of depression and panic. When the Soul of man is free, it carries him through Red Seas and desert experiences to the Promised Land of spiritual peace. Freedom is a condition of the Soul. As we turn to the kingdom of our inner Self, we find the reign of divine Power in the outer world. As we seek peace within, we find harmony without. We reach the depth of the Soul, and It takes over our existence, providing activity and newness of life, a peace and serenity, the like of which we have never dreamed. We then have achieved the freedom of the Soul, the freedom of grace.

All through the ages there have been spiritually endowed men and women—the mystics of the world—who have known conscious union with God, and who have brought the presence and power of God into their actual experience. Always there has been a Moses, an Elijah, a Jesus, a John, or a Paul, but none of them had many followers. None of them was ever widely known or his teaching widely practiced, during his own time or for years afterward. These spiritual masters devoted their lives to giving us the truth which has brought us to our present state of consciousness. The light that we have today is the result of the light which has come down through all time. There are many spiritual teachers who have left no record, and about whom we have no knowledge; but there are many whom we can identify: Moses, Elijah, Jesus, John, and Paul, mentioned above; Eckhart, Boehme, Fox, and other mystics of the twelfth to the seventeenth centuries; as well as the great leaders and revelators of more recent years. No one person has given the light to the world, but each of these great spiritual prophets has been a beam of light contributing to the whole light.

These great spiritual leaders are all in agreement on the basic principles and teachings with which most of us are acquainted: Thou shalt love the Lord thy God with all thy heart; thou shalt do unto others as thou wouldst have others do unto you; thou shalt not kill; thou shalt not steal; thou shalt not commit adultery. They did not teach that we all be of the same nationality, color, or creed; they taught the principle of love and co-operation. If this principle of love and co-operation were really practiced and lived by the millions of people who accept the teachings of the Christ, war would be an impossibility. It is a paradox that, thousands of years after these revelations of truth, strife and struggle continue to be the motivating force in the world. With this vast reservoir of mystical wisdom available, we should expect that after all these years the world would be enjoying freedom and abundance. But the principles of these teachings have not always been practiced as they were revealed; instead they have been crystallized into form, and gradually they were adulterated, sinking at times to the lowest level of human thinking rather than rising to the heights to which these truths ultimately lead.

The original principle taught by the Master Christian revealed that the kingdom of God, the presence and power of God, is within. Jesus called this presence and power "Father"—"the Father that dwelleth in me, he doeth the works." Paul, using a different term, said, "I can do all things through Christ which strengtheneth me." By whatever name It is called—God, Father, or the Christ—It is to be found within. The kingdom of God is within us; the whole of the Godhead is to be found within our individual being, not in holy mountains nor yet in the temple at Jerusalem, but *within us*. If we really believed this great wisdom, we should be willing to leave the world for a season, until such time as we could reach, touch, and respond to the Father within. As we begin to recognize our good as the gift of God, we let the reasoning, thinking, planning mind relax. We listen for the still small voice, ever watching for the angel of the Lord, the Christ, the Father within. It will never leave us nor forsake us. It is our permanent dispensation.

This listening is the art of meditation, in the learning of which we come to a place of transition where truth leaves the mind and enters the heart. In other words, there is no longer merely an intellectual knowledge about truth; but truth becomes a living thing within our being. To illustrate: Everybody in the world knows the word "God," but there are few people in the world who know *God*. For most of us God has remained a word, a term, a power outside the self; God, Itself, has not become a living reality except to those few people who are known as mystics. Meditation leads us to an experience in which we know that there is a God. It leads us to a point where we are as convinced of the reality of God as we are of the fact that we are here reading this book. If all the newspapers in the United States carried headlines tonight saying that we were not in this place at this particular time, this announcement would not alter our knowledge of the fact that *we are here*. God is as much of a reality, as much of a presence, as much of a power, as much of an entity and individuality as we are, and God can be just as well known by us as we can know ourselves or one another.

From the moment that we know God through experience, life changes for us, because there is a relaxation of our personal selfhood. A feeling arises of something other than ourselves operating in us, through us, and for us—something greater than ourselves. This has been the experience of all mystics. They have actually known God; they have felt God's presence; and God has become an active power in their lives. There are not many of such people in the world. If there were but a few more who really knew God, perhaps those few might be enough to save the world. According to Scripture, ten righteous men have saved a city. The mystics' conscious awareness of the presence and power of God is the product of experience: it is not mere conversation about God's availability; it is not only an affirmation or a statement; it is not merely a platitude or a cliché; it is a living fact.

Our search for God, our seeking the kingdom of God, is an evidence of our own faith in the presence and power of God, even though we do not yet have a knowledge of it through actual experience. Those who are not on the spiritual path do not have that confidence. Only those who have attained an inner conviction that there is a God are led to the search for God. These seekers may not necessarily have attained the realization of God, but at least there is that inner certainty: "This is the way; there *is* a God."

So the search begins, and it begins in different ways. How it begins depends upon our background; it depends upon where we happen to be at any given moment and what is going on in our particular world around us. There have been people whose search began in orthodox churches and some of them have found the answer there. They have discovered the kingdom within themselves, but have continued working in the church as a form of service and sometimes as a form of gratitude. Some have found God through an intellectual approach, and a few have found a purely spiritual way. Others have come through teachings that are a combination of the intellectual and the spiritual. There are those who have come to the spiritual path through books, and there are those who have come through living teachers, while others have made contact with the spiritual saints and seers who have never died.

To know the truth as so many words, quotations, passages, or theories is one thing; but it is an entirely different thing when, through meditation, the Word takes root in our consciousness and comes forth as spiritual fruitage. We are told that the fruits of the Spirit are "love, joy, peace, long-suffering, gentleness, goodness, faith." It is really true that when the Spirit has been touched or when It has touched us, then the fruitage comes forth in the form of harmony, wholeness, completeness, and perfection. The purpose of this book is to help students practice the art of meditation by which the Word takes root, so that they come into an actual awareness, an actual consciousness of living in the Spirit. Our object is to attain a measure of that mind which was in Christ Jesus, and then let It do with us what It will. It is to reach that consciousness in which Paul revealed, "I live yet not I, Christ liveth my life"; or "I can do all things through Christ which strengtheneth me." In other words, the activity of the Spirit comes alive in us, and It takes over: we are no longer good and we are no longer bad; we are no longer sick, but neither are we well. We are at a stage which transcends the pairs of opposites.

In spiritual wisdom there are no pairs of opposites. God is, and, therefore, there is no concern as to whether or not we can reach God, because there is nothing for which we need to reach God: the day is already beautiful; the fruit is already on the trees; the flowers are already blooming; the tides are flowing; the sun and the moon and the stars are in the heavens; harmony is. In this state of spiritual consciousness we come to that place where we rest and relax in the realization, "God's in his heaven—all's right with the world!" In that realization, we withdraw from the struggle for the things of this earth.

"Let this mind be in you which was also in Christ Jesus

. . . he that raised up Christ from the dead shall also quicken your mortal bodies by his Spirit that dwelleth in you." We must seek the attainment of that same Spirit that raised up Jesus from the dead, not by talking about it, or declaring it to be so, not teaching or preaching it—but by having that mind. The attaining of that mind requires effort, plus the grace of God. The grace of God is the most important factor, because without it, no one would have the fortitude to continue on the path leading to God-realization. Without the grace of God, no one would have the desire even to begin the search, let alone to pursue the arduous steps which must follow.

There is an area of consciousness revealed in meditation through which we are instantly one with God and with all spiritual being and creation, and through which we find all forms of good instantly available. This area of consciousness has been described as a Sea of Spirit, the universal or divine Soul, the Father within. In achieving conscious contact with this Sea of Spirit or the Father within, we find divine Love pouring Itself into expression, so that we no longer live by personal effort alone, but by grace. Rather than seeking our good from persons or things, we tap this universal Soul and become beholders of Its activity, pouring forth as the ideas which become the human forms of good necessary to our present experience. It is only as we learn to look within to this Infinite Invisible that we begin to understand the nature of grace.

Instead of seeking or desiring something already existing as form or effect, let us learn to turn within and let our good unfold from the divine Source, the Infinite Unseen. Let the business and professional man look to the Divine within; let the sick and the sinner seek healing and perfection from within. Let each one of us ever be alert, watching consciousness unfold as new and richer forms of good, experiencing the abundance of life—by grace. To understand that Soul is the eternal storehouse of all good is to permit the activity of the Christ to function in our experience. Let us draw our good from the infinity of our own being, from the kingdom within. Touching that center, the Father reveals our heritage as "heirs of God and joint-heirs with Christ" to all the heavenly riches. This is to live by grace, the gift of God. The children of God always live by grace.

The secret of grace is contact with the Infinite Invisible, the universal center of being within us. This is the experience of the Christ. In mystical literature, this spiritual experience is called Illumination, Cosmic Consciousness, or Christ-Consciousness; in the New Testament, it is spoken of as being "born again," or rebirth. Reading and studying inspirational literature and scripture, as well as frequent pondering and meditating on God and God's creation, lead to actual communion with the Father, which brings to our consciousness this touch of the Christ. Keeping the mind stayed on God leads to an awareness; sometimes, there is even a voice, and we know that "he performeth the thing that is appointed for me to do." Those who have attained this light have no further problems of existence, since now they are fed, clothed, and housed by the infinite fountain of life which we call the Christ. This moment of grace cannot be adequately described, since it appears in different ways to different people; but all who have received this light understand the experiences of the illumined of all ages.

The activity of the Christ, resulting in a life by grace, is by no means limited to the past. Today, many men and women are experiencing the Christ and are living lives of beauty, health, harmony, and joy—by grace. With truth now available to all who can read, spiritual illumination is a possibility to every earnest seeker. "Acquaint now thyself with him and be at peace." The awareness of the Father within is the beginning of a life by grace.

To live by grace enables us to do greater things and to achieve better results in all our activities. This spiritual impulsion and divine guidance permit us to drop all concern

for our personal welfare, or for that of our families or nation.
Freedom from fear, danger, or lack comes only as the Comforter appears. The voice of Truth utters Itself within us, and
It becomes the "peace be still" to every storm in our
experience. It is as if there were a Presence always going
before us to "make the crooked place straight," to make
the desert "blossom as the rose," and to open the doors
of opportunity, service, and welcome. As the activity of the
Christ is manifested by greater and still greater deeds of
spiritual power, our trust and faith grow by leaps and
bounds. Secure in this inner conviction, the struggle against
every form of discord ceases, and we live "not by might nor
by power, but by my Spirit"—by grace.

A few people are born into the world with some measure
of Christ-consciousness, but anyone with sufficient perseverance, application, and fidelity may develop and cultivate a
Christ-awareness, that "mind which was also in Christ Jesus."
It does, however, require devotion, consecration, and a
receptivity which recognizes and welcomes the Christ as It
touches and awakens our Soul into newness of life. In the
silence of our being the Christ speaks and we hear, "I will
never leave thee, nor forsake thee. . . . I am with you alway,
even unto the end of the world." This consciousness of
God's presence is developed by patience and perseverance,
in quietness and stillness, and by abstaining from the use of
mental power or physical might, so that the Spirit may function. "Be still, and know that I am God."

"For by grace are ye saved through faith; and that not
of yourselves: it is the gift of God. . . ." By grace are *you*
saved.

THE WAYS

To every man there openeth
A Way, and Ways, and a Way,
And the High Soul climbs the High Way,
And the Low Soul gropes the Low,
And in between, on the misty flats,

The rest drift to and fro.
But to every man there openeth
A High Way, and a Low,
And every man decideth
The Way his soul shall go.

—John Oxenham*

* From *Selected Poems of John Oxenham*, edited by Charles L. Wallis (Harper, 1948). Used by permission of Miss Erica Oxenham and Harper & Brothers.

CHAPTER II

THE PURPOSE

The purpose of meditation is to attain divine grace. Once this grace has been attained in a measure, it takes over our experience and lives our life, performs those things which are given us to do, and makes the crooked places straight. We no longer live by bread alone, but by this inner grace.

Satisfying relationships, abundant supply, successful business activity, and creative endeavor are the tangible effects of grace. First must come the inner grace before the things of this world can be added to us; but we can never receive the grace of God so long as we seek it for the purpose of demonstration, that is, seeking God in order to possess some person or thing, or to achieve some place. That is the reason meditation can never be *used* to demonstrate an automobile, more money, or a better position: meditation is for the purpose of realizing God. In meditation God is revealed *as* the life of individual being. God is the embodiment of all good. In achieving the experience of God, our good appears as whatever the need may be. We fail if we attempt to gain any thing separate and apart from God. God, Itself, is the good. Prayer or meditation for material things and persons cannot be answered by a God of Spirit. Such an objective defeats the purpose of meditation.

Scripture tells us that the natural man receiveth not the things of God. Who is the natural man but the human being, the prodigal son, still deep in material consciousness, praying that his materiality may be made a little better, a little richer, a little more, or a little less? We pray to be stouter or we pray to be thinner; we pray to have more money, seldom to have less, although that might be a very spiritual prayer. The point is that we pray for an improvement or an increase of that very materiality of which God has no knowledge, and such prayer is not answered. Very often our human desires, if fulfilled, would leave us unsatisfied, because as human beings we do not possess the wisdom to know the things of which we have need. It is the Father within who is all wisdom and all love.

To be effective, prayer must be addressed to a God of Spirit, and, therefore, that for which we pray must be of a spiritual nature. Let us remember this every time we turn to God in meditation; let us measure the quality of our prayer by the degree of spiritual illumination we are seeking, and from that we shall know whether or not we may expect fulfillment. "I am come that they might have life, and that they might have it more abundantly." The promise is fulfillment, but let us be sure that the fulfillment for which we are praying is a spiritual fulfillment, and then we shall not pray to a spiritual God to improve our humanhood; but we shall obey the scriptural injunction to let the Spirit bear witness within us: "for we know not what we should pray for as we ought; but the Spirit itself maketh intercession for us. . . ."

It is not really we who pray or meditate at all; the Spirit meditates within us, and we simply open our consciousness to let the Spirit reveal our need and its fulfillment. Therein is the secret. How different that is from doing mental work, declaring or affirming that this or that shall come to pass—

and now, this minute. Rather, in going into meditation, our attitude should be that of the little Hebrew boy, "Speak, Lord, for thy servant heareth." That is the true attitude with which to enter into meditation—opening our consciousness to God and letting God fulfill Itself within us. Let God utter Its Word within our being—not our words, but the Word. We shall find that Word to be quick and sharp and powerful; it does not return unto us void. It does the work whereunto it is sent, but it must be the Word of God, not your desire or my desire. The true aspirant on the spiritual path has no desire other than the fulfillment of God, the realization of God, the experience of the Christ. How could there possibly be an unfufilled need if the Christ is operating in our consciousness? The Christ must fulfill Itself. One desire alone is legitimate and that is the realization of this activity of the Christ in our consciousness.

"The Father within me, he doeth the works." The Father is within me and the Father is within you; then why is it that the works are not done? There is one thing needful, and that is our conscious realization of Omnipresence. The activity of God is within us, the presence of God, the power of God; but we have built up a state of consciousness consisting of layers and layers of material sense. We have not succeeded in breaking through these layers to reach the atmosphere and altitude of God within us and, until we do so, we shall fail in our meditation and miss the path to fulfillment.

Most of us come to the search for God with a purely material outlook on life: concerned that the heart beat so many times a minute, that the digestive and eliminative organs function in a prescribed way, that our supply consist of so many dollars; always believing that satisfaction can be found in the external world. Some believe that money will bring that satisfaction; some believe that fame is the answer; still others believe that fulfillment lies in good health. How often is it said: "If only this pain could be stopped, then I really could begin the search for God. I can't do it while I am in such pain," or "If only my rent were taken care of, then I could be at peace and would be able to search for God." In other words, these people are implying that the realization of God is dependent upon some physical or financial condition. Evidence to the contrary is the fact that there are people with millions of dollars who have not discovered God; there are people in perfect health who have not known God; nor have they found either completeness, peace, or fulfillment. That is the state of consciousness of most of us as we come to the search for truth. Let us reverse the picture: Let us begin the search for God; and in finding God, see the pain disappear; watch the lack, the limitation, and the sin vanish.

As long as we are merely trying to exchange physical discord for physical harmony, we can have no conception of what the kingdom of God is, of spiritual riches, or of spiritual health. We must begin our meditation with the recognition that neither health nor wealth is the object of our search for God. Any desire for things or persons will prevent or delay our entrance into the spiritual kingdom, but the steadfast remembrance that the goal we are seeking is God-realization will open the way and make a highway for our God. In that realization, we find all things added unto us, or to be more accurate, we find all things included within us.

We must realize that we have no objective other than the achievement of the kingdom of God, that we have no demonstration to make except the demonstration of our spiritual Selfhood; but *that* we must demonstrate: first of all, for our own development; and secondly, as a witness to the world that God is individual Selfhood, and that this state of being may be attained by all those who are ready to give up the world, not by removing themselves to some remote spot, but by giving up their desires for that which the world can give.

As students of spiritual wisdom, the important question is: What is the best way, if there is a best way, of achieving this realization of our true Selfhood? Is there a short cut? Is there a path that leads to God-realization, a path that can be trod here on earth? Can it be achieved here on earth? And the answer is yes. Not only is there a way of accomplishing this objective, but there is a short cut. That short cut, so simple and yet so very difficult, is to perform a bit of mental surgery on ourselves and cut away all our desires. Let us take a good sharp scalpel and cut out of ourselves all desire for person, place, thing, circumstance, or condition. Every desire must be cut away in order that only one remains: to know Thee, whom to know aright is life eternal.

Let us set our whole heart and soul and mind on the realization of God rather than on the attainment of some form of good. As we attain that realization, we enjoy all the good things of life which come forth, without becoming slaves to them or becoming attached to them and without fear of losing them. No one can ever lose his wealth, his health, or his life once he has attained a touch of the Christ. Let our prayer be:

One thing have I desired, that I might know Thee. One thing! My heart cries out, "God, open Yourself to me, reveal Yourself to me. I care not whether You reveal Yourself in wealth or in health, in poverty or in sickness; only reveal Thyself. In Thy Presence is security, safety, peace, and joy."

In meditation we are seeking the grace of God and nothing but the grace of God. This grace is not found in the human mind, nor is it found in such peace as the world can give. Making statements and reading books about it do not bring it forth. These may be of assistance in leading us to a point where we are prepared in the silence to receive the grace of God, but it is meditation which lifts us to a state of spiritual apprehension where divine grace takes over. "If so be that the Spirit of God dwell in you," then are we children of God. As human beings, we are cut off from

God and for that reason do not come under the law of God and do not experience the blessings of God's presence and power. It is the Son of God, the spiritual image and likeness, which is held in the bosom of the Father. We have wandered away from our Father's household and squandered our divine substance in a personal sense of "I." Now, in order to realize our sonship with God, we must take the path of return to the Father's house—that same journey the prodigal son had to make—that we may be clothed with the robe and receive again the jewel of adoption.

How do we become the Sons of God? How do we awaken the Christ, or Son of God, which always has been, is, and always will be our true identity, even though it has been hidden from sight during this period of mortality in which we are sleeping? To do this requires effort. We must abandon all our previous concepts of life "for my name's sake." We must get up from the banquet with the swine, leave behind all thoughts, people, and activities of the swinish world, and return to the Father. It is the nature of the human being to love self-indulgence: ease, comfort, riches, intemperance, gluttony, indolence, and sensuality. These operate in our consciousness as a sense of separation from God. It is not actually separation from God, because we can no more be separated from God than a gold ring can be separated from the gold of which it is formed. Gold is the ring; gold constitutes the ring. There is no possible way to remove the gold from the ring without destroying the ring, because there is not gold *and* a ring; there is only a gold ring.

So it is with us. We cannot be separated from God, because there is no *we*. Actually, there is no such thing in all the world as you or me as individuals standing alone. God being infinite, God is all there is. God constitutes you and me; God constitutes our life, mind, soul, and being, just as gold constitutes the ring. Gold is the substance; the ring is the form. God is the substance; the individual is the form *as* which God appears. God is the essence of our being—the life, soul, mind, spirit, law, continuity, and activity. God is the all and all of individual being, whether of saint or sinner. The degree of sainthood expressed by an individual is wholly dependent upon the degree of conscious realization of oneness with the Father. The capacity for sin in an individual is dependent upon the degree of his sense of separation from God. As a matter of fact, this sense of separation is all there is to humanhood.

We are not human beings as we seem to be; we are pure spiritual being. It is not that there are two separate beings, the human being and the spiritual being; it is only that a human being is entertaining a sense of separation from God. We cannot be separated from God, but we can entertain a *sense* of separation from God. The moment that sense of separation begins to disappear, Christhood or divine sonship is revealed. The return of the prodigal takes place wholly within one's self as an activity of consciousness, and the moment one sets his feet in the direction of the Father's house, he has entered the spiritual path.

Let no one take credit for being on the spiritual path. Were it not for the grace of God, one would not be reaching out toward the realization of his divine sonship. In the experience of every person, there comes a certain moment when he is penetrated by a ray of God, when a touch of God breaks through into his consciousness, not because of himself, but in spite of himself. From the moment that ray touches him, the end is inevitable: he will find his way right to the throne of God.

To human sense, the spiritual way of life seems impossible of achievement, ephemeral, and intangible. But in reality, the most tangible thing, the most real thing in all the world is Spirit or God. Once this is perceived, the things of this world—the dollar bills we use for exchange, our homes, and our relationships—take their rightful place as outer symbols of grace or effects of Spirit. It is these symbols or effects which change. As long as men and women live by bread alone, by the strife and struggle involved in human activity; as long as they are dependent exclusively on symbols or effects, they will discover eventually that these worldly possessions waste away, are consumed, and become as nothing. We see the results of a dependence on material things as we look into the faces of the men and women who are living by these effects, placing their reliance on the health of their bodies, the wealth of their pocket-books, and the things of this world.

In contrast with these people, a few stand out, here and there, who have an inner light by which they live, an inner hope, expectation, or glory. This spiritual light is easily detected: We see it in the eyes; we hear it in the voice; we observe it in the vitality and vigor of the body. Although this Presence is invisible, It is within every person; no one in the world is without It; It is available to everyone who has ears to hear and eyes to see, to everyone who is receptive to divine grace.

The whole purpose of our existence is to be a fitting instrument through which God's glory may appear. We shall never fulfill ourselves in life by trying to express *our* individuality; fulfillment lies in letting the Infinite Invisible bring Itself through into expression. Then we do not strive and struggle to glorify ourselves, but every time we meditate, it is as if we were to say:

Father, "I can of mine own self do nothing. . . . My doctrine is not mine, but his that sent me." I have no wisdom of my own, Father; I have no power; I have no judgment; I have no health; and I have no wealth of my own. I am sitting here to let infinity flow.

Our function is to abide in that inner realization and let harmony appear. As our vision is on the unfolding of the Christ, It appears outwardly as a better, healthier, or wealthier human being. But we are not deceived by appearances, because we are not looking for a change in the human picture. Meditation is not an attempt to turn sickness into health or lack into abundance. The vision always is on the one invisible Christ at the center of our being, here and now.

Any meditation that has within itself a single trace of a desire to get something from God or to acquire something through God is no longer meditation. Good is to be realized, yes, but not to be achieved: the infinity of good is already where I am; the kingdom of God is within me. Locked up inside of our being is the presence and power of God, the whole of the Godhead, just as perfume is locked up in a flower. As the flower opens the perfume or the fragrance escapes. Everyone has the allness of the Godhead locked up within his own being—not just a part of it. God cannot be divided; God is indivisible. God is infinite, but God is indivisible. The allness of God is in one tiny leaf—in every leaf: the allness of God is in every individual on the face of the globe. Were this not true, there would have been less of God on earth when the population was only 10 per cent of what it is today, and, by the same token, there would be twice as much of God on earth when the population is doubled. No, there was just as much of God in the world a million years ago as there will be a million years hence. The infinite allness of God is wherever one individual is. That is why it is said that one Christ Jesus can lead a million people into heaven, because one Christ Jesus is the infinite individual Son of God and shows forth all that God is. "Son, thou art ever with me and all that I have is thine" is not addressed to a group but to an individual. God, in Its infinite allness, is embodied in the Son of God, in whom is our spiritual identity. As we learn to turn within and let this imprisoned perfume escape—this activity of the Christ, this beauty of God—then does it come into visible being.

When we no longer search for the peace that the world can give, but seek only "my peace," the gates of consciousness open to admit the spiritual light which becomes the life of our being and our body. Many people desire spiritual power in order to enjoy more harmonious experiences. Their purpose in seeking God usually is to enjoy more and better earthly things, to catch larger fish in their nets—bigger fish, better fish. But the basis of our work is to "leave your nets," to leave this search for more and better human good and open consciousness to the spiritual realities. Then the things which come to us in the outer world are the fruits of an inward grace. Grace can only be attained by a state of inner silence, a state of inner awareness and receptivity; therefore it is necessary for us to prepare ourselves for the experience of receiving that grace. This is the whole purpose of meditation.

The amount of illumined force and power that flows through us is determined by divine grace. Whether or not we reach the final goal of illumination is not our problem. Some will seek and strive until they exhaust themselves and yet will not attain it; others will go along easily and steadily; and a few will spontaneously burst out all over with the springtime of the Christ-consciousness. The experience of the Christ is one that is achieved purely through grace. In whatever degree it comes, it comes as the gift of God. It does not come because we earn it; it does not come because we deserve it; it does not come primarily because we are good men or women—in fact, it is often likely to come to the sinful one, because the inner struggle of the sinner may be greater than the struggle of the good man, and such a struggle is often highly rewarded.

The only responsibility that we have is that our desire be for the Christ-experience, and that that desire be shown forth by the sincerity of our study and the depth of our meditation and devotion. That is the extent of our responsibility. The Christ-experience is purely the gift of God. No one earns it; no one deserves it; and no one knows why it comes to some and why it does not come to others.

In the experience of every earnest student, there comes a period of initiation; that is, there comes a period of the opening of the soul. It may be achieved through something that is heard, something that is read, or it may come through direct contact with the consciousness of a spiritual teacher. When it comes, the student needs no further help from sources outside of himself. His entire teaching is received from within: his entire illumination, healing power, and regenerative power come from within. From that moment on, he becomes a blessing to others along his way, bringing healing and comfort to them. As he goes deeper into the Spirit, he awakens in them this same Christhood: "I, if I be lifted up, shall draw all men unto me." In proportion as any individual receives spiritual light, that light becomes a law unto those who are within his orbit. Everyone who has ever brought about a healing through spiritual means has been the light, and it was the light in his consciousness that brought about the healing. Whatever degree of light we realize, automatically makes us, in that degree, a light to all those who touch our consciousness. That is the purpose of meditation: that each one may attain a higher degree of that light through the experience of the Christ.

Once we have achieved this contact with our inner Being, we are free: we are in bondage to no man, no circumstance, no condition. We are free in Christ and we can then say:

Christ liveth my life. What difference does it make whether or not there are periods of depression or periods of prosperity, floods or droughts? Christ liveth my life. It leadeth me beside the still waters; It maketh me to lie down in green pastures. A thousand may fall at my left hand and ten thousand at my right hand; still it will not come nigh me. I have made that contact. I am dying daily to my human-hood; I am being reborn of the Spirit; I am being guided, directed, fed, maintained, sustained, healed, and saved by this inner light—this inner illumination.

The secret is the awakening of the sleeping Christ, and that is the purpose of meditation.

CHAPTER III

THE PRACTICE

There are many forms of meditation leading to the awakening of the sleeping Christ within. There is no one way suitable to all people. Each person must ultimately find the way which appeals to his particular consciousness. All methods call forth that deep sense of humility which knows "I can of mine own self do nothing." Satisfactory meditation requires a letting go of personal selfhood, with its egotistic claim to possessing a wisdom of its own, in order that the Power which we call the Father within can take over. This Power is within us, not within our body, but within our consciousness, and through meditation we permit It to escape from within, that It may act on the without and become the saviour to our experience.

The initial stage of meditation may be a contemplation of God: the beauty of God's universe, the law of God, and the activity of God. Our life becomes that of a beholder, beholding the glory of God in all things—in the green grass, in the gentle breeze, in the turbulence of the ocean, and in the calm of the night. In this contemplative state of being, we cannot behold anything in this world, without at the same moment recognizing its cause, the invisible spiritual activity, which produced it. We should never look at a sunrise or a sunset, without instantly realizing the spiritual nature of that which brought it into expression— God, the creative Principle of the mountains, the skies, and the seas; God, the creative Principle of that which fills the air with birds and stocks the seas with fish. If we live continuously in the contemplation of the invisible Presence and Power underlying all things, this very place whereon we stand is holy ground.

As we ponder the glory of God, contemplate His wonders, our mind is stayed on God. Fewer and fewer extraneous thoughts thrust themselves upon our consciousness. We are able to sit for many minutes, sometimes for as long as an hour, finding ourselves at peace in our contemplation of God and the beauty of the spiritual universe. Contemplation lifts our consciousness into an atmosphere of receptivity, into a consciousness where miracles can take place. The conscious thinking mind comes to a stop, and the invisible Presence and Power is given an opportunity to function. Until that It, that invisible Selfhood, that invisible Presence and Power, is permitted to operate in consciousness, we are merely functioning on the mental level.

The human mind cannot be the avenue for the activity of the Soul: a higher consciousness must be reached. Through this higher consciousness, through that mind which was in Christ Jesus, the Soul reveals Itself and Its activity as our individual experience. That which imparts itself to us from the inner consciousness is power, not the thoughts we think, not our statements or beliefs; but that which reveals itself from within on the inner plane is the power, with signs following. This inner consciousness is without boundary, and, by rising to a higher level of consciousness, we become aware of that which lies far beyond our immediate knowledge. This higher consciousness is unlimited and imparts its wisdom to us infinitely and eternally. It is that insulated place within our own being, where the ceaseless activity of the outer world does not intrude.

If we are faithful in the practice of contemplation and the simpler forms of meditation, this practice will lead us from one form of meditation to another, until we arrive at the actual experience of hearing the still small voice, of receiving divine guidance from within, and of being divinely led every step of the way.

Let us begin by sitting in a comfortable position. Some people prefer a straight chair, even a hard one, so that they are compelled to sit in an upright position; whereas others find themselves more comfortable in an armchair. Keep the feet flat on the floor; hold the body erect, with the hands resting in the lap. In this natural, relaxed, but alert position, begin your meditation with some passage of scripture that may come to your thought, or, if you like, you may open the Bible or a book of spiritual wisdom and read for a short time. You may read only one paragraph, or you may need to read ten pages before some particular thought attracts your attention. When this occurs, close your book and take that thought into your meditation. Think about it; hold it right in front of you; repeat it to yourself. Ask yourself: Why did this particular quotation come to me? Does it have an inner meaning? What is its significance to me at this time?

As you continue meditating another statement may come to your attention. Consider both of these thoughts: Is there any relationship between them? Is there any coherence? Why did this quotation follow the first one? By this time probably a third idea and then a fourth will have come, and all these thoughts will have come out of your awareness, out of your consciousness. In this short period of meditation which may have been of only a minute's duration, you have experienced God revealing Itself; you have opened yourself to divine Intelligence and Love. This is the Word of God which is quick and sharp and powerful.

To have received one statement of truth from the depths of our own being is evidence that we have had a degree of realization of God; peace and quiet descend upon us; and a sense of well-being and assurance well up within us. This form of meditation, if practiced faithfully, opens our consciousness to permit God to function in our life, to permit Christ to live our life—*but it must be practiced*. It is necessary, therefore, to return to our meditation at our first opportunity, and to repeat the process in the middle of the day and again in the evening. We may find that we are unable to sleep continuously throughout the night. In the middle of the night, the demand comes, "Meditate."

These periods of silence, reflection, introspection, meditation, and finally communion prepare us to receive the inner grace. Even though we seem to be making no progress in these three- or four-minute periods of meditation during the day or night, even though we seem to feel no response, let us not become discouraged, because we have no way of judging the results of our efforts in terms of a single period of meditation or even after a week or a month of this practice. To expect immediate results from the practice of meditation would be the same as expecting to play Bach or Beethoven after the first music lesson. Would it not be absurd, after the first six hours of practicing the scales, to give up in despair, because we have not achieved immediate proficiency in an art which requires a high degree of technical skill? If we were serious in our desire to master this art, we would recognize that from the moment we began the practice of our scales, something was taking place in both mind and muscle. It might require a whole year of practice before any degree of skill was attained. The final achievement cannot be measured in terms of the hourly or daily or even monthly periods of practice.

So it is with meditation. We have made a beginning the very first time that we close our eyes and realize:

I am seeking the grace of God; I am seeking the Word that proceedeth out of the mouth of God. I know not what to pray for, so I do not pray for anything of this world. I listen for Thy voice. I wait for Thy Word.

This form of meditation repeated a dozen times a day would eventually change our entire life, and it is possible that changes might be evident within a month. Every time we turn to that inner center, we are recognizing that we, of our own self, can do nothing; we are seeking the kingdom within. This is true humility, true prayer, an acknowledgment of the nothingness of human wisdom, human power, and human strength. It is acknowledging that wisdom, power, and strength come from the Infinite Invisible. These periods of silence create an atmosphere of Spirit in which the activity of Spirit, without our knowing it or having any awareness of it, goes before us to make the desert blossom as the rose.

Here is an example of a simple form of meditation in which we begin with a central idea, theme, or quotation and ponder it until its inner meaning is revealed:

"I can of mine own self do nothing. . . . The Father within me, he doeth the works." The meaning of the first part is immediately apparent; but what is meant by the statement that the Father within me doeth the works? What is the Father within me? Who is this Father within me? We know that when Jesus made that statement he was referring to God. It must mean, then, that God within me doeth the works. Jesus said that it is your Father and my Father, so he seems to be telling me that there is a God-power—something within that doeth the works. The same Father that was in Christ Jesus is also in me. This Father within me, this He, is greater than he that is in the world, greater than the problems of the world. The Life, Intelligence, and Wisdom that is within me is greater than he that is in the world, greater than my enemies, greater than my

ills, greater than my ignorance, greater than my fears, greater than my doubts, even greater than my sins.

"I can do all things through Christ which strengtheneth me." This Christ is the Father within me, the divine Power within, which Jesus said "will never leave thee nor forsake thee." The Father within, the Christ which strengtheneth me, will never leave me nor forsake me. Before Abraham was, this Father was within me, and It is with me even unto the end of the world. It is a Presence and a Power that has been with me from the beginning of time, even when I did not know It was there, and It will be with me throughout all eternity.

It will be with me regardless of where I am: If I make my bed in hell, . . . if I walk through the valley of the shadow of death, . . . this Father is ever with me. It is a Presence that never leaves me, a Power that always strengthens me, that goes before me to make the crooked places straight and the rough places plain. I feel Thy hand in mine. I know. I know that there is a Power that can do all things. I know that there is a Presence that can live my life for me, make my decisions, and show me the path of life. The whole kingdom of God is within me. Thou wilt never leave me nor forsake me; I can never doubt thy Presence. All this Thou hast revealed to me from within myself.

I thank Thee, Father, that Thou hast hid these things from the wise and prudent and hast revealed them to me, a babe in truth, a beginner on the spiritual path.

This practice of pondering a scriptural quotation is not too difficult for a beginner or too simple for an advanced student. As in the example given above, a central thought or quotation is used in an attempt to understand its inner meaning and to receive light on it, so that never again will it be used as a quotation or as a metaphysical cliché. These primary forms of meditation should be understood and practiced before the higher, more difficult forms are attempted.

Let us remember that our object is to develop a state of receptivity to the still small voice. In meditation we do not think about our problem; we turn within and wait and wait and wait. We wait for three, four, or five minutes. If, at the end of that time, we have not felt a response within ourselves, we get up and go about our customary duties. An hour or two later we again meditate, waiting silently—waiting until the voice of God utters Itself within us. The thoughts that race through our mind do not concern us; we are not interested in them. We are waiting until we feel the activity of the Christ stirring within us. If we do not feel the touch of the Christ within three or four minutes, we return to our daily tasks, but two or three hours later we meditate again. If it is necessary, we continue this practice for years; but if we are persistent, the day will come when there will be an inner response, which will give us the assurance that there is that within us which the Master called "the Father," that which Paul knew as "the Christ."

The beginner should meditate three times a day or, if that is not possible, at least twice a day, in the morning and at night. There is no one who should find this too difficult to do, because everybody gets up and everybody goes to bed. Everybody can spare a few extra minutes in the morning and at night, even if he cannot find one other minute for this purpose during the twenty-four hours. For serious students, however, there will always be another interval sometime during the day. Gradually, these periods of meditation become a regular part of our existence, and we are meditating at any or every hour of the day or night, sometimes for only half a second or for several minutes at a time; sometimes while driving a car or doing housework. We learn to open consciousness, if it is but for a second, and find ourselves in a state of receptivity.

Take any aspect or facet of spiritual truth. It might be the term "light." There have been innumerable people who might be called "the light of the world." Jesus was that light, as were Elijah, Paul, and John. But what is meant by the phrase "the light of the world"? Let us turn to the Father and ask Him to give us light on the subject of "light." As we develop the listening ear, we gain the spiritual sense of the term rather than the literal meaning as given in the dictionary or the interpretation given to it by some metaphysical writer. We then have our own God-given light on the subject of "light."

Perhaps the meaning of the word "Soul" is not clear. Very few know what Soul really means; it is one of the most profound mysteries of spiritual wisdom. To understand it, let us turn to the Father for a revelation on the subject of the Soul. Sooner or later as we maintain a state of receptivity, we shall begin to receive impartations on the nature of the Soul. In this way we learn to take into our consciousness any word or subject about which we are seeking understanding, and to wait, in a state of expectancy, for the light to shine on it and reveal its meaning to us.

Most of us are familiar with the passage, "My grace is sufficient unto thee." We know the words, but they will be of little or no significance in our lives unless their inner meaning is revealed through meditation. Only then do these words live for us and become the Word. When we awaken in the morning, we should consciously bring to remembrance the statement that God's grace is our sufficiency in all things. We do not repeat it over and over again, as a vain repetition or affirmation, but rather do we take this statement into consciousness and dwell on it:

Thy grace is my sufficiency—Thy grace—yes, the Father's grace within me. The Father is within me, and it is the Father's grace that is my sufficiency in all things. Now I know whose grace it is; but what is grace? What do we mean by grace? What is it?

It may take two or three minutes for us to perceive that "Thy grace" is not afar off, but is within. That may be the extent of the unfoldment for the moment. Two or three hours later, however, we again bring this statement to conscious remembrance. This time we may recall that we were considering the word "grace." It will not be long before we begin to realize that we have heard grace described as the gift of God, as that which comes from God without our earning it, deserving it, or laboring for it; it is something which comes without personal effort. This grace, therefore, which is to be our sufficiency in all things, is an activity of God within us.

In meditation the meaning of grace may be revealed to one of us in one way, and to another in an entirely different way; but to both, it may come with such force as to open the windows of heaven and pour out "a blessing that there shall not be room enough to receive it." To each one something different will unfold from that which is given to anyone else.

If we are in earnest, we shall take the statement "My grace is sufficient unto thee" into consciousness many times during the day. If we abide in that statement of truth we shall be meditating and thus fulfilling one of the most important teachings that has ever been given to the human race: "If ye abide in me, and my words abide in you, ye shall ask what ye will, and it shall be done unto you." If we keep the Word alive in our consciousness by dwelling on it four, five, eight, ten, twelve times a day, and also when we awaken in the middle of the night, we shall find that we are meditating. We are letting the Word of truth abide in us and Christ becomes the activity of our consciousness.

What is Christ? If you really desire to know what the Christ is, begin with this very humble acknowledgment: "Father, I know so little about the Christ; help me to understand the Christ." Then close your eyes and keep your attention on the idea of the Christ. Every time the mind tries to wander, gently bring it back. Keep your attention centered on the Christ. Ultimately, you will catch the vision of the real meaning of the Christ, a meaning that you will never quite be able to explain to anyone else; but you, yourself, will know it. The Christ will be an actual presence in your consciousness; It will be a power, an influence, a being. Yet, It will be something that you cannot define. No matter what you might say about the Christ, It would not be that.

One day, however, as you persist in this meditation, the Christ is alive in your heart and then you hear:

I *will never leave thee. As I was with Moses, so I will be with you. Whithersoever thou goest, I will go; I will be right there with you. Only remember to look for Me; expect Me. Do not look for any sign; do not look for anything outside. Look only to Me. If you look only to Me, one day when you think you need water, it will come out of a rock, or when you think you need food, it will come out of the sky—but never look for it. That is the sin—looking for it. Look only to Me. I am walking beside you. I am sitting within you. I am resting in your heart. I am in your mind, in your consciousness. I am right here in your arms, down in your finger tips. Do you feel Me? I am with you. I go before you to make the crooked places straight. I will never leave you. Look unto Me and be saved. Seek Me while I may be found, and all these things shall be added unto you. Seek Me.*

From the moment that awareness is ours, we have demonstrated Paul's statement, "I live; yet not I, but Christ liveth in me." Then, this atmosphere of the Christ is with us always, and our very physical presence becomes a benediction to everyone with whom we come in contact. Because we are there? No, because the Christ is there as the light of our being. The way is to pray without ceasing. We consciously open ourselves to the realization of the Christ until the time comes when you and I no longer have to do it consciously, because there is no longer a you or an I to do it. Look unto *Me,* the Christ, and be ye saved.

CHAPTER IV

THE INDISSOLUBLE UNION

Very little progress can be made on the spiritual path of life until we have caught some vision of what God is, of what our relationship to God is, and of what God's function is in our life. This cannot be a vicarious experience; it must be individual and it must be approached in a completely relaxed manner. We must be unwilling to accept any authority other than our own interior revelation. So we ask ourselves questions about God, which will lead into a meditation on God: What is God? What does God mean to me? What is the place and function of God in my life?

How many people have ever had a God-experience? How many have felt the flow of the Spirit in their minds, in their souls, in their bodies? The number is small, only a few hundred or at the most a few thousand in a generation; and yet God is available to every man, woman, and child. God demands our entire love and devotion; we must give ourselves to Him in order that He may reveal the eternal givingness of Himself to us. We must love God supremely with our whole heart, mind, and soul; love God so much that our only prayer is: "I must feel God; I must let God fill my soul, my heart, my mind, my being, my very body."

We speak of God as impersonal Intelligence, Mind, Principle, but God is personal, too. The relationship between an individual and God is closer than his relationship with his own mother. It is like reaching out and feeling a presence always there, gentle, reassuring in its very quietness; it is joy, peace, and warmth. The moment we have a God-experience, that gentleness is there, that peace is there, that warmth is there; and with it comes a love toward everything in this world, a sense of companionship and joy in one another.

The normal concept of God is that of a God separate and apart from us, who has within Himself all good but is withholding it from us. Usually, in praying to God, it is for the purpose of seeking or getting something from God—health, supply, opportunity, companionship. Most of us believe that God possesses this good, but for some inexplicable reason is withholding it from us, and so we pray to God to bestow some of it upon us. Sometimes, if our prayers are not answered quickly enough, we make all sorts of promises in a futile attempt to bargain with God—promises which often we have no intention of keeping.

In a vain effort to reconcile a supposedly loving God with a God who turns a deaf ear to our supplications, we often censure ourselves, believing that some evil act of omission or commission is the reason God is withholding good from us. Some physicians contend that many of the ills of the world, both mental and physical, are the result of guilt complexes. Countless people live in a state of gnawing self-condemnation, consumed by a sense of guilt; sometimes for some serious offense committed in their past, but more often for some small or inconsequential act. If we believe that we are being punished by a vengeful God, our concept of God is entirely erroneous, because God has no memory of our faults and failings; God is too pure to behold iniquity; God has not punished and does not punish sinners. The sinner is punished by his own sin, not by God. Even the confirmed sinner knows that there are certain laws of God which must not be violated. He knows that if he violates these laws, punishment follows, but what he does not know is that that punishment is not God-inflicted, but self-inflicted.

God is not a vindictive God; God is not a withholding God, but neither is He a giving God. God is Love and He neither withholds nor punishes; there is no love in withholding and there is no love in punishment. If God waited for us to be good or deserving, if He waited for us to find the right words with which to placate Him, if He waited for us to use a form of meditation or method of treatment which would be pleasing in His eyes before He was willing to bestow His blessings upon us, He would be a cruel and capricious God. God will never give more than He is giving us now. God is forever being God: God is being life; God is being love; and God is forever expressing Its life and Its love.

James says, "Ye ask, and receive not, because ye ask amiss." Every time we turn to God for something, expecting to get something from God, we pray amiss. No one has to tell God to make the grass green or the roses red; no one has to tell God when to make the stars shine or when to change the tides. Shall we, then, presume to tell God that we are in need of anything? God *is* the infinite Intelligence of this universe. If our God knows how to produce a pearl in an oyster or petroleum in the earth, if our God knows how to direct the birds in their flight and to cover the earth with Its wonder and glory, is not this same infinite Intelligence sufficient to be the governing and guiding influence in our experience without our proffering any advice, information, or suggestions?

The basis of all meditation and prayer must be an understanding of the nature of God and of our relationship to God. God is eternal Life, infinite Intelligence, divine Love, but "I and my Father are one . . . and he that seeth me seeth him that sent me." It is God, the Father; and God, the Son; forever one. As we relax in that realization, It takes over and

It functions harmoniously, joyously, abundantly. The very moment, however, that we turn to God with any sense of getting, desiring, or even hoping, we prevent God's operation in our experience, because we are injecting our finite concepts and views which interfere with the flow of God. When we refuse to entertain any concept of what God's will should be, when we stand in the divine Presence, pure of heart, with no finite will, no personal desires, hopes, or ambitions; then, we go to God with clean hands and a pure heart and we can say, with conviction and trust: "Thy will be done in earth, as it is in heaven. I am Thine; Thou art mine. I am in Thee; and Thou art in me. Thy will be done in me."

Far too many people in the world doubt God's love or they would not be spending so much time praying for God's bounties. If they really believed that God is divine Intelligence and Love, why should it be necessary to try to advise or influence God? God *is*. What greater prayer is there than those two words? What could better lead us into the interior kingdom of our own being? Satisfactory meditation comes with the absolute conviction that God *is*: that God is Intelligence and Love; that there is no power apart from God and no power in opposition to God. There is nothing interfering with the expression of God's love for His children. Thy grace is my sufficiency in all things is the acknowledgment of the presence, the wisdom, the love, and the power of God in our experience. Watch what happens as we begin to accept this kind of God and no longer reach out to something outside ourselves, but merely stand still in being and say, "God is."

God is a state of Being, a state of infinite Intelligence and ever-present Love. The life of God cannot be lengthened nor can it be shortened; the life of God cannot age nor can it change: God is a state of eternal, immortal, infinite Being. ". . . God is light, and in him is no darkness at all. . . . And God is able to make all grace abound toward you; that ye, always having all sufficiency in all things, may abound to every good work." That should be our attitude in entering into meditation.

The acknowledgment of divine grace is meditation. It is a recognition of the nature of God and of our relationship to God. That relationship is oneness. We are the children of God, co-existent with God: "And if children, then heirs; heirs of God, and joint-heirs with Christ. . . ." Our heavenly Father knoweth our needs, but sometimes we pray as if we were poor insignificant creatures, who must prostrate ourselves before some great and terrifying deific being who holds our fate in his hands, and not very tenderly at that. At other times, we outline the manner in which our needs are to be met, believing that we can influence God to act in accordance with our desires. What we must do is to acknowledge God, acknowledge the all-knowingness of infinite Wisdom, the all-lovingness of all-encompassing Love, the all-power of that which knows no other power than Its own infinite nature and being—but let us not ask for a translation of this into human terms. Let our meditation be the recognition of God, Itself, and we shall find that that will suffice.

God is one: one Power, one Law, one Substance, one Cause. This teaching of oneness is probably the highest spiritual teaching ever given to the world. The entire ministry of the Master, Christ Jesus, was based on the old Hebrew teaching of the idea of God as one: "Hear, O Israel, the Lord our God, the Lord is one." According to Genesis, in the beginning God created the world and all that therein is. Anything that God did not create was not created, was not made. In the light of this truth there is only one Substance and because there is only one Substance, there is no substance to be destroyed, to be healed, or to be improved. There is only one Law, and, therefore, we cannot use the law of God to destroy any other law or its effects. When we understand God as Life, there is only one Life and we can never have a life to save, or a life to heal or redeem. There is only one.

Now that we know all these things about God, let us look

at them as landmarks along the road we have been traveling, but landmarks we have long since passed; and let us forget all of them. No one is ever going to find God until he is stripped of all his concepts of God, until he leaves behind every synonym for God he has ever heard and launches forth into the unknown to discover the Unknowable. There is no such thing as a thought about God or a concept of God that is correct, because a concept always remains a concept.

How, then, do we arrive at a realization of what God is? After we have become well-grounded in the letter of truth, there comes a time when we must be willing to admit that all our knowledge about God has been in the realm of the intellect, and that nothing we can know with the mind is absolute truth. Nothing that we can think about God is truth; nothing we can read in a book about God is truth, because these represent merely limited, human opinions about God. To John, God was revealed as Love, but we cannot accept that as truth, because we do not know what love is in the sense in which John understood and used the term. To Jesus, God was Father, because the deeper meaning of that word was revealed within the consciousness of Jesus. The realization of God must come as an individual unfoldment to every aspirant on the spiritual path.

During the years of my own unfoldment it was necessary for me to let these commonly accepted synonyms for God drop away one by one, because it was not possible for me to know what those who revealed them meant by their use of these terms. When every concept had been brushed aside, I was left with the term "the Infinite Invisible." Why "the Infinite Invisible"? Because the Infinite Invisible did not mean anything that I could understand. Neither you nor I can grasp the Infinite; neither you nor I can see the Invisible. The Infinite Invisible is a term that denotes something which cannot be comprehended by the finite mind. That does not mean, however, that the Infinite Invisible is the correct term for God. It is correct for me, because it provides me with a term which my mind cannot encompass. That satisfies me. If I could grasp the meaning of the Infinite Invisible, it would be within the range of my human comprehension, and I do not want that kind of a God.

God cannot be known with the human mind, but if we listen and are still, in that stillness, God reveals Itself. Right where we are God is. ". . . Whither shall I flee from thy presence? . . . if I make my bed in hell, behold thou art there." The presence of God is within our consciousness. We do not have to reach out for God even mentally, or pursue God as if He were afar off or as if He were something difficult to attain. Many have found as they gave up their frantic search for God, learned to be still, and ceased the parrotlike repetition of meaningless words and phrases, that one day there came an awakening and they discovered that God had been right there beside them all the time, quietly whispering, "Wait—why don't you stop and let *Me* have something to say?" How would that *Me* speak to us in a moment of helplessness, if we were out on a desert, lost, with no way for us to find human help, and no way for human help to find us? As we listen. we hear Its whispered words:

The place whereon I stand is holy ground. Whither shall I flee from thy Spirit? "Yea, though I walk through the valley of the shadow of death, I will fear no evil: for thou art with me." Alone, yet not alone; helpless, yet not helpless; divine help is here where I am, and it does not have to find me, and I do not have to find it. God is here where I am. The kingdom of God is within me, for I and the Father are one. God is not lost, and I am sure God has not lost me. If I am here, God is also here.

This is a powerful meditation. We have not asked, begged, or pleaded for anything. We have recognized the truth known to Jesus, John, Paul, Moses, and Elijah, the truth every one of them revealed, that where I am, God is. It is a universal teaching that has been known to every master and spiritual teacher throughout the ages, but it has been lost through the worship of a far-off God and through the belief that God and His beloved Son are separate beings.

In this meditation we realize that God is within our own being, but not confined within the limits of our flesh. No surgeon can operate and find God, yet God is within our own consciousness, closer than breathing and nearer than hands and feet. If we are ever in a place of discord, let us never forget that our salvation is closer than breathing, because I and the Father are one.

Look at that statement, "I and my Father are one." Visualize a figure one and see contained in that figure one the Father, the Son, and the Holy Ghost. That one is God, the Creative Principle, invisible; that one is the Son, appearing as the figure one; that one is the invisible Holy Ghost, which maintains and sustains the Son throughout all eternity. That one never becomes a two; it never becomes a minus one, because there is something inherent in it that maintains its oneness.

Just so every person is one with God. That oneness includes God, the Father; the Son, the individual identity; and the Holy Ghost, the activity of God, which maintains and sustains this oneness, the individual identity, called Ruth, Robert, or Joel. That which we see is not all there is to Ruth, Robert, or Joel; there is more than the eyes behold, because right where this form appears is the creative Principle, the sustaining Activity. There is an individual identity called Robert: Robert, the Son; plus Robert, the Father; plus the Holy Ghost—God, the Father; God, the Son; God, the Holy Ghost. This breaks down every sense of separation from God. The activity of God maintains each individual identity unto eternity, supports it, feeds it, sustains it, and bestows upon it Its abundance, success, and grace. Let us stand still and be fed, maintained, sustained, and directed by this invisible

Force, whose function it is to be the Messiah.

The purpose of this meditation is to arrive at the real meaning of oneness, the inner meaning of the statement, "I and my Father are one." Let us center our attention on this statement. Sometimes we may find it difficult to hold our attention to one thread of thought for any length of time, but if we lose the thread, we can gently come back to it in this way:

"I and my Father are one." As a wave is one with the ocean, so am I one with God; as a sunbeam is an emanation of the sun itself, so am I one with God. Therefore, I can never be lost. I can never be alone. The presence of God is here where I am, in this very place where I find myself, even though I call it hell. In the valley of the shadow of death, I shall not fear, for God is with me.

I will never leave you nor forsake you. Before Abraham was I am. Before Abraham was, I was with you, and I will be with you unto the end of the world. I in the midst of thee am mighty: I in thee and thou in me and we are one. Whithersoever thou goest, I will go; whithersoever thou goest—east or west, north or south, in the sky above or the sea below—whithersoever thou goest, I will go. I will never leave thee nor forsake thee. If you walk through the waters, you will not drown, for I am with thee. If you go through the fiery furnace, the flames will not kindle upon you, for I am with thee.

The nature of God is I. Quietly, humbly realize that that I whom you have thought to be you, that I whom you have thought to have problems is God. How then can you—that I —have problems or know limitation? If you believe that God is your Father and my Father, and that that Father is within you, how far can you ever be from guidance, from protection, from supply? When you realize the nature of God to be I— from then on, I have no problems.

It is not likely that any of us will be faced with the un-
usual situation of being lost on a desert, but let us never
doubt for a moment that at some time or other we shall find
ourselves in some kind of a wilderness only to discover that
God appears to us as manna from the sky, water from a rock,
or the opening of a sea. From Genesis to Revelation, the
Bible is the history of your life and of mine. In some degree,
whatever happened to Moses will happen to us; whatever
happened to Elijah, to Jesus, to John, to Paul, will, in some
measure, take place in our experience. We may be in some
wilderness only to learn that where we are God is, that the
place whereon we stand is holy ground. The voice of the Lord
will direct us in the way we should go. We shall not hear this
direction if we believe that the voice of God was reserved
for Jesus, Isaiah, Elijah, or Moses, two or three thousand
years ago. We are able to hear it only if we can accept God as
one: God, the universal Father; and God, the Son.

All meditation on God is fruitless, unless we realize that
what is true of God is true of us as infinite individual being.
Only as we establish the infinite nature of God's being as the
nature of individual being, do we complete the realization
that brings harmony into our experience.

The nature of God is *I*, that *I* which dwells in the midst
of us, that *I* which we recognize to be individualized as our
own being. This *I* is not the body we see with our eyes; it is
not the egotistical "I" which believes that a human being
has all power or that a human being is God; but it is that
gentle *I* which looks out from the center of our being. The
human self-centered "I" must "die daily" that the divine *I*
may be born again in us, and our divine relationship be revealed.

God is individual being. God is your being; God is my
being; God is the being of every form of life—human, animal,
vegetable, mineral. God *is individual being*. God is the law,
the life, the soul, the substance of individual being, and,
therefore, all that God is, I am: "all that the Father hath is

mine." That is beautiful scripture, but it is of no practical value unless we become living embodiments of that principle.

God is my individual being; God constitutes my being; God is the life, the soul of my being, the spirit. God is the very substance of which my body is formed. God is the only law governing me—not laws of lack or limitation; not laws of food, climate, or digestion; not laws of medical belief or theological belief—God is the only law. God's law is a law of immortality, eternality, and perfection; it is self-maintained and self-sustained.

Temptation to believe that we have a being separate and apart from God may come to us in one form or another. The temptation may come when a call for healing reaches us. Our first response may be, "Oh, I haven't enough understanding." If we are alert to recognize the truth of God as individual being, we shall realize:

Of course, I haven't enough understanding and I never shall have enough understanding to heal anyone or anything. Health does not come through my understanding. This health must come as the activity of the Christ, not because of my understanding—not because of what I know, or do not know. I am a willing instrument, Father. I am willing to be still; I am willing to let the activity of Thy being be my being and Thy grace the sufficiency unto this individual or this situation. "I can of mine own self do nothing. . . ." I, the Son, am but the instrument for I, the Father.

God, alone, is the source and fount of all that is: of all supply, of all health, and of all relationships. If we use our money as if it were being taken from our own storehouse, we shall find our supply reduced by just that much; unless we have recognized that this money does not really belong to us—it belongs to God, because "the earth is the Lord's and the fullness thereof." All supply is in and of God. When we spend, therefore, let us spend as if it were God's abundance and not ours that we are using. Then we shall find that we do not have less—instead there will be twelve baskets full left over. This was the principle the Master was illustrating when he multiplied the loaves and fishes.

The Bible teaches that the earth is the Lord's and the fullness thereof. Even while we are repeating such words, however, many of us still believe that God's abundance is something separate and apart from us, and that at some point or other there is a transfer action where that which belongs to God becomes ours. This is as ludicrous as thinking that the beautiful flowers growing in our garden belong to us. All nature would laugh at such an idea. God is the source of every flower that blooms in a garden. God is the source of everything. What difference does it make whether the fullness of the Lord blooms as a flower or as a dollar? There is no point of transfer between that which is in God and that which is in us. All that is in God is in us at this very moment, because "I and my Father are one"—God, the Father, the creative Principle, invisible; God, the Son, the visible; and God, the invisible Holy Ghost, the maintaining and sustaining influence.

This is the teaching of the Master: to "deny thyself" or to "die daily." This is the teaching of Paul: to let mortality be dropped so that we may be clothed with immortality and God be revealed in all Its glory as individual being. As long as there is a personal "I" attempting to achieve anything, accomplish anything, get anything; there is a selfhood struggling to maintain itself, separate and apart from God. But it *is* possible to die daily; it *is* possible to deny self, because the only denying of self is a denial that I can of myself be or have anything: that I can of myself be good; that I can of myself be spiritual; that I can of myself have spiritual power; that I can of myself have health; or that I can of myself have wealth. That is the only denying of self there is, and that is dying daily. It is ceasing to try to gain something for ourselves. The lesson itself is easy: Let us not desire to add more fish, bigger fish, or better fish to our nets. Let us deny that we have any need of fish, because all the fish in the sea belong to God, and everything that belongs to God belongs to us. In denying the personal sense of self, we glorify the Self which we really are—the God-Self. The God-Self is our true being, and the measure of our Selfhood is infinity.

In recognizing God as individual being, we are recognizing infinity at the center of our own being, an infinity which we can permit to flow out from us to the world. The very moment, however, that a thought of getting, acquiring, demonstrating, or achieving anything enters our thoughts, we block or prevent this infinity from escaping. When we recognize that we are but the instrument for Its entrance into human consciousness, then, we carry with us the spiritual, holy atmosphere of the allness of God within our very being. Without a trace of egotism, with no desire for personal glory or profit, we realize that anyone, anywhere, who in sincerity comes to us for God's grace, can receive it. God's grace is a sufficiency unto the situation—not our knowledge or possessions. Then in peace and in quietness the flow begins to pour out from us as warmth, as release, as joy. To be able to be still and know that the "I" of us is God, that that God is our individual being—interior selfhood, internal nature, character, and quality—and that all that God is, is flowing out from us into visible manifestation and expression as us, automatically sets us free.

When our relationship to God is established, we can travel the world over without purse and without scrip. We can begin each and every day anew with nothing and in a short time find our every need fulfilled. We, humanly, shall not be desiring to acquire or achieve it, but we shall be living the principle:

God is my individual being. *All that the Father is, I am; all that the Father hath is embodied within my consciousness. It does not come to me; I am but the instrument through*

*which it flows to those who are not yet aware of this great
truth of their relationship to God.*

Wherever the need is, there is fulfillment. Fulfillment
exists in consciousness as the consciousness of individual
being, and that consciousness is God. Fulfillment involves
a transition in consciousness. It may require days, weeks, or
months of meditation before we come to the realization that
God is individual being and that the place whereon we
stand is holy ground. Never again can there be a need or desire, without its being instantly fulfilled from within, as the
fulfillment of consciousness. God is our consciousness; God
fulfills Itself, daily and hourly, in every form necessary. The
basis of this realization is God as individual being.

Since God is individual consciousness, we can, with faith-
fulness, persistence, and perseverance, reach the kingdom
of God within us and bring it forth into our experience, so
that it takes over our entire life. This God-consciousness
can fulfill Itself only in proportion as we nullify the personal
sense of "I." Going to God without a single desire eliminates
the "I" in large measure, because it is only the personal "I"
who could have a wish, a desire, or a will. We turn to God
to receive a spiritual blessing or benediction, and no one
knows what will be the nature of his particular spiritual blessing or benediction. "Eye hath not seen, nor ear heard, neither
have entered into the heart of man, the things which God
hath prepared for them that love him. But God hath revealed
them unto us by his Spirit."

When the Finger of God touches us, It may place us in a
completely different life—if that be Its destiny for us. For
each of us there is a destiny; we are not all intended to engage in the same kind of activity:

Now there are diversities of gifts, but the same Spirit. . . .
And there are diversities of operations; but it is the same God
which worketh all in all. . . .

For to one is given by the Spirit, the word of wisdom; to another the word of knowledge, by the same Spirit;

To another the working of miracles; to another prophecy; to another discerning of spirits; to another divers kinds of tongues; to another the interpretation of tongues;

But all these worketh that one and the selfsame Spirit, dividing to every man severally as he will.

For as the body is one, and hath many members, and all the members of that one body, being many, are one body; so also is Christ.

God works as bridge builders, coal miners, teachers, salesmen, lawyers, artists, ministers; and it is God, the infinite Intelligence, at the center of our being, which determines our special form of expression. To know what Its destiny is for us, we must touch this center within us in meditation.

The degree of fulfillment experienced is in proportion to the degree of consciousness unfolding. Wherever we are at this moment in life represents the degree of God-life unfolded in conscious expression, and we can change that expression by opening our consciousness for a greater flow. Those who open themselves to God through meditation are at one with the Infinite Invisible. God uses the mind, soul, and body as instruments for Its activity and unfoldment, and the grace of God flowing through them is a benediction to the world:

"My grace is sufficient for thee." Thy grace is not only my sufficiency, but Thy grace is the sufficiency of all those who come within range of my thought. Father, I am an instrument through which this invisible blessing may appear in the world for those who seek Thee. The kingdom of God is within me, the kingdom of righteousness; it is Thy kingdom and Thy power and Thy grace. Thy grace is a blessing and a benediction to all who are in the world. It is my joy that this blessing—this benediction of God, this grace of God—

shall flow equally to friend or foe, near or far, that it shall flow to those of any nationality, race, or faith who lift their hearts to God. It is my joy that all those who honestly lift their thought or voice to God shall find their benediction and blessing through Thy grace which flows through me.

CHAPTER V

THE DIFFICULTIES

If we practice the foregoing meditations faithfully, undoubtedly many questions will arise as to certain procedures in meditation: What about the extraneous thoughts that race through the mind? Should we expect to see visions? Is there a definite length of time for each meditation? How much understanding is necessary? Does diet have any bearing on the effectiveness of meditation? Is any particular posture necessary or desirable?

Let us consider the question of posture first. Meditation is most easily practiced when we are not conscious of the body. It we sit in a straight chair, with feet placed squarely on the floor, the back straight as it normally should be, the chin in, and both hands resting in the lap, the body should not intrude itself into our thoughts. This normal and natural position we should be able to maintain for five, ten, or twenty minutes, without thought reverting to the body.

There is nothing mysterious about posture. In the Orient, few people sit on chairs; therefore, it is natural for them to meditate sitting on the floor with their legs crossed. In that position, they are comfortable; but we, of the Occident, would find such posture not only difficult to achieve, but, for most of us, very uncomfortable to maintain.

If it is remembered that in meditation our whole attention is to be focused on God and the things of God, it will be readily understood that in meditating it is wise for the body to be in a natural or comfortable position, so that the attention is not drawn to the body. The only reason for assuming any particular posture is to make it easier to center the attention on God and to become receptive to Its infinite power. In meditation, a change within the system is noticeable. The spine is erect; the chest is high; the breathing becomes slower, and thoughts race through the mind less and less until they finally cease.

Meditation is a conscious experience. As suggested earlier, it is a great help to begin meditation with some question, thought, or specific idea on which we wish enlightenment. We begin with the idea of receiving an unfoldment from God. If we realize that meditation is a conscious activity of our Soul, there will be no danger of our falling asleep or becoming drowsy. Two or three minutes of meditation should be enough to drive away the weariness one sometimes feels at the end of a strenuous day's work. We cannot go to sleep with a mind open, waiting for instruction. Those who fall asleep during meditation fail to make it a conscious experience. At a certain stage of meditation, sleep may come, but such sleep is not a lapsing into unconsciousness. The activity of consciousness would continue during sleep. Meditation is not just a lazy sitting back and saying, "All right, God, you go ahead." It is a quickening alertness and yet it is the "peace that passeth understanding."

Let us be sure there is that peace. We must make certain that there is no strain in connection with meditation. We are not going to take the kingdom of God by force—by mental or physical power. When meditation begins to be an effort, stop it; or we shall defeat our purpose. It is not necessary to meditate for any specific period of time. If the meditation has been of only one minute's duration, let us be satisfied, because if we have been keeping our mind stayed on God for but half a minute, we have started the flow.

Meditation is a difficult art to master. Were it not so difficult, the whole world would long ago have mastered its technique. In my own experience, eight months of from five to ten meditations a day were necessary, before I received the very first "click" or sense of the Presence within—eight months of meditating day and night. Furthermore, I had no knowledge that such a thing as making a contact with God was possible, or that it would accomplish anything once it was achieved. There was, however, deep within me, an unwavering conviction that it was possible to touch something greater than myself, to merge with a higher power. Nobody whom I knew had gone that way before me; nobody had prepared the ground for me. There was only that inner conviction that if I could touch God, at the center of my being, It would take hold of my life, my work, my practice, and my patients. By the end of eight months, I was able to achieve one second of realization—perhaps it was not even one second. I do not know how to measure time when it involves less than a second, but it certainly was less than a second of realization. It was another week before the next second of realization came, and many days before the third one. A whole week intervened before the fourth moment of realization was achieved; then, it happened twice in one day. Finally, the day came when the realization seemed to last for an eternity and that eternity was certainly far less than a minute. It was probably three years before I learned that if I got up at four o'clock, sometime between then and eight in the morning, I would feel that "click" or awareness that God is on the field. Some days the "click" came within five minutes and some days it took the whole four hours, but never after that did I leave for my office until the Presence had been realized.

Now there are never less than nine or ten hours out of

the twenty-four given over to meditation—not in one single period, but five minutes at a time, ten minutes, twenty minutes, thirty minutes. There is no regular schedule: Sometimes I go to bed at eight o'clock in the evening, get up at about ten-thirty, and meditate from then until three o'clock; then back to bed again until four or four-thirty, up again and in meditation until dawn. Moreover, whenever anyone comes to see me, after I have let him talk for a few minutes, we meditate. This is the way—constant, constant meditation, a constant turning within so that the inner impulse is kept fresh.

As we advance in this work, if we permit ourselves to be deprived of our periods of contemplation, by the pressure of business or the demands of increasing responsibility, we shall miss the way. Once the Christ-center has been touched, it is possible that outer activities may increase to such an extent that they encroach upon the time which should be devoted to meditation. Too great an indulgence in the things of this world might soon take from us the spiritual gift which is infinitely more valuable than any material thing we may sacrifice. The Master withdrew from the multitudes to commune alone in the wilderness and on the mountaintop. We, too, must withdraw from our families, our friends, and our human obligations for those periods of communion necessary to our inner development and unfoldment. An hour or two of meditation or communion, with no purpose or desire of any kind, brings the experience of God to us in an ever-deepening measure.

Frequently the question of diet in relation to meditation is raised. Is there any special diet which, if followed, will enhance one's spiritual capacity? Are certain foods to be avoided by the aspirant on the spiritual path? Should one refrain from the eating of meat?

At every stage of our unfoldment we are tempted to believe that something we do or think in the human realm will help us in the development of our spiritual awareness. This is a false assumption. On the contrary, it is the development of our spiritual awareness that changes our every-day habits and mode of living. As the aspirant progresses along the spiritual path, he may find himself eating less and less meat and, ultimately, may reach the point of being unable to eat any meat at all. Let us not, however, believe that there is virtue in some act of omission or commission, that some form of material sacrifice will increase our spirituality. Spirituality is developed through the reading of spiritual literature, the hearing of spiritual wisdom, the association with those on the spiritual path, and through the practice of meditation. The kingdom of God is found by inner realization. The outer transformation in one's dietary habits is a direct result of an inner spiritual grace; it is a result of the spiritualizing process taking place in consciousness. Abstaining from the eating of meat is not a means of developing inner spiritual grace; but the development of inner spiritual grace leads to the renunciation of such things on the outer plane.

Another question that arises is in regard to psychic visions. Are such manifestations a desirable or necessary part of the experience of meditation? Psychic visions, such as seeing colors or being confronted with an apparition of a supernatural character, may have some relevancy to our human experience, but remember this: they are entirely on the psychic level or in the mental realm of consciousness. In spiritual literature, these visions are never referred to or considered as spiritual experiences. Psychic experiences have nothing to do with the world of Spirit. The psychic world of seeing visions, colors, or anything of that nature is left behind in the realization that right here and now we are spiritual beings, the manifestation of all that God is. For that reason, let us not linger in the psychic realm, but rise above it into the pure atmosphere of Spirit.

Many times in meditation we attain a sense of peace or harmony—the realization of the presence of the Christ. These are inspiring experiences, but we must be willing to give up even that deep peace and rise to the next higher level of consciousness in which the attaining of that peace is of no significance or importance whatsoever. Having realized the everpresence of the Christ, is it necessary to have any kind of an emotional reaction? Whether we feel emotionally satisfied or emotionally starved will make no difference, since we shall have realized that the activity of the Spirit is an eternal thing, always with us.

One of the greatest hindrances to meditation is the fear that we do not have enough understanding with which to begin this practice. The Psalmist forever disposed of such fear and doubt when, in the 147th Psalm, his heart and lips sang forth the praises of God: "Great is our Lord, and of great power: his understanding is infinite." It is *His* understanding, not ours, which is important. Let us give up all this nonsense about our not having enough understanding or about our having such a great understanding. We must remember, it is *His* understanding. In quietness and confidence, therefore, let us turn within to let truth reveal itself. There is no limit to understanding, if our dependence is on God's understanding rather than on our own. There is not a person reading this book who does not have sufficient understanding to begin the practice of meditation and, thereby, enter the kingdom of God. By grace, even the thief on the cross was enabled to enter paradise "this day," and we, too, by grace can enter the gates of heaven at this very moment.

The major difficulty with meditation is, of course, the inability to hold the thought in one direction. This is neither your fault nor mine, but is partially the result of the accelerated tempo of modern living. The infant is given a rattle, and as soon as he outgrows that he is given another toy. His entire attention from infancy through adolescence and into adulthood is centered on people and things, so that if he ever found himself alone, he would be overcome by fright. Most people have never learned how to sit down by themselves and be quiet; many of them have never learned how to be quiet long enough even to read a book. Our culture has focused attention on the things of the world to such an extent that we have lost the capacity to sit quietly and ponder an idea.

When we close our eyes in an attempt to meditate, we are amazed to discover a boiler factory inside of us. All sorts of thoughts flash through our minds, simple things such as: Did I disconnect the electric iron? Did I turn on the refrigerator? Did I put the cat outside? Other thoughts, not so simple or unimportant, come in—thoughts of fear or doubt. Let us not be afraid of these thoughts; they are world thoughts. We are like antennas picking up all the broadcasts of the world. If we disregard these world thoughts, in a few days or weeks they will die for lack of feeding. Only as we accept them as our thoughts, do we feed them.

Although our object is to attain a quietness and receptivity, we should never try to still the human mind; never try to stop thinking or to blank out our thoughts. It cannot be done. When we begin to meditate and thoughts of an unruly nature come, we should remember that they are world thoughts, not our thoughts. Let them come. We will sit back and watch them, see them impersonally. Eventually they will stop, and we will be at peace. As often as our thought wanders in meditation, we gently come back, with no impatience, to the subject of the meditation. There will come a time, as we continue in this practice, when these extraneous thoughts will not impinge on our consciousness. We will have starved them by neglect. We will have made ourselves so unreceptive to them by not fighting them that they will not return to plague us. But if we fight them, they will be with us forever.

In meditation we must be very patient in our endeavor to conquer any sense of unrest. No truth that we do not already know is going to be given to us from without, but the light presented on that truth from within our own Soul makes it applicable in our experience. Truth that comes from without is a mere semblance of truth; it is the truth revealed within our own consciousness which becomes the "light of the world" to all who come within range of it. "I, if I be lifted up from the earth, will draw all men unto me." Meditation will lift us to the point where we apprehend the word of truth in its inner significance. The rhythm of the universe takes possession of us. We do not move; we do not think; but we feel that we are in tune, that there is a rhythm to life, that there is a harmony of being. This is more than peace of mind; this is the spiritual peace which passeth understanding.

In order to enter into the mystical life, we must master the ability to remain in the silence without thought. This is the most difficult part of all spiritual practice. In no way is this a cessation or repression of thought, or an effort toward such; instead, it is such a deep communion with God that thought stops of its own accord. In that moment of silence, we begin to understand that the divine mind, or cosmic consciousness, is an infinite intelligence imbued with love, and it functions as our being, when conscious thinking has been stilled.

In our everyday life, we may have one plan in mind and the cosmic mind may have another, but we shall never know its plan so long as we are busily engaged in thinking, scheming, and reacting to the activities and distractions of the world. To receive the divine grace of the cosmic mind, there must be periods when the human mind is in a state of quiescence. The individual who is master of his destiny has reached the state of consciousness where nothing in this world is of any importance to him. Only that is significant which takes place when he has risen above the sea of thought. In that high place the divine thought, the divine activity of consciousness, reveals itself. This does not mean that our mind must or will become a total blank, but it does mean that throughout the day and night we must have several periods of time in which there is no desire other than the joy of communion with God. It is in this complete stillness and respite from thinking that the Father takes over in our experience.

Before we can enter the mystical life, the habit of con-tinuously thinking and talking must be transformed into the habit of continuously listening. Our Master spent much of his time in silent meditation and communion, and we may be assured that he was not asking God for anything of a material nature. He was not talking; he was listening. He was listening for God's direction and instruction, for God's guidance and support.

It is in developing that listening ability and receptivity that the human mind is quieted and becomes stilled to such a degree that it is an avenue or instrument through which God manifests and expresses Itself. This human mind, this reason-ing, thinking mind, is not to be put off or destroyed. It has its place. It is not consciousness, but it is a facet of con-sciousness, an avenue of awareness through which we re-ceive knowledge and wisdom from consciousness.

Thinking is an initial step leading toward meditation. Let us suppose that we are not advanced to the place where we live in a constant state of receptivity. True, God is always uttering His voice, but we are not always listening. Thought may be used to help us reach that exalted state of listening consciousness, but in meditation no thought should be used in the sense of an affirmation or denial.

Let us suppose that we desire to meditate, but the human mind is in such a turmoil that we do not find ourselves im-mediately in a state of quiet and peace. Instead of attempting to blank the mind and blot out these disturbing thoughts, we use the mind and turn to scripture or to some other book for inspiration. Now let us see how this operates in the use of such a quotation as "Be still and know that I am God." The student who has learned to rely on affirmations would repeat over and over again, "Be still and know that I am God. Be still and know that I am God. Be still and know that I am God," until he reached a point of self-hypnosis and, in that state, temporarily found himself still. To repeat continuously, "Be still and know that I am God," is nothing but suggestive therapy, nothing but affirmation and denial used to hypnotize oneself. It is not spiritual practice; it is not spiritual power. Some people have become so hypnotized through the use of such an affirmation that they actually believe that they, as human beings, are God.

Now let us take that same statement, but instead of using it as an affirmation, let us discover its real meaning through meditation:

"Be still and know that I am God." What does that mean? Of course, you know, Joel,* that you are not God. So what does this mean? It says, "I am God," not that Joel is God. That is quite different. I, yes, "I and the Father are one. . . . God in the midst of me is mighty. . . . I and the Father are one." Yes, Joel and I, the Father, are one. The Father and Joel are one; right where I am, God is—closer than breathing, nearer than hands or feet. Be still, Joel, because the I in you is God. You do not have to seek protection, help, or healing anywhere. I am with you. Be still and know that that I is your protection, your salvation, your security.

In the contemplation of this scriptural passage, peace enfolds us and we are at rest in a divine stillness.

A few on the spiritual path achieve this stillness quickly and easily, but for most, the Way is long and difficult. It is not for any of us, however, to boast about the rapidity of our progress nor to decry its slowness, but to pursue the way with steadfastness and unswerving purpose. Most of us have periods of gradual progression, punctuated by interludes of desolation, when we feel that we have lost the way and are wandering in a maze of conflict and contradiction. Often we find that, after these valley experiences, we go forward to new heights where unsuspected vistas spread out before us.

There are a few gifted individuals who, because of pre-

* The reader may insert his own name in using this meditation.

vious experiences, have been so well prepared that their way seems to be much easier than others'. The purity of consciousness which they have developed makes the ascent into spiritual consciousness a beautiful, gradual, and harmonious journey beset with very few problems.

For most of us the path is up and down, but by the end of a year or two there is usually a feeling that we are a trace ahead of where we were the year before. The prerequisite for the hearing of the still small voice, for the actual experience of the Christ, is to prepare ourselves by study, meditation, and by mingling with others on the spiritual path. When we hear the still small voice within us, we have received God's grace, and the purpose of meditation is being achieved.

We dare not be satisfied with anything less than the experience of God Itself. It is the pearl of great price. It is for each of us to decide how much time and effort will be given over to meditation: to determine whether we will spend a few spare minutes now and then or so arrange our lives as to permit prolonged periods of uninterrupted quiet in which to contact the inner Presence and Power. The years necessary to the study and practice of meditation are not years of sacrifice to the aspirant; rather are they years of devotion to that which is his goal in life. It requires patience, endurance, and determination, but if the realization of God is the motivating force in our lives, what the world calls a sacrifice of time or effort is not a sacrifice, but the most intense joy.

PART TWO

MEDITATION:

THE EXPERIENCE

THE MEDITATION OF MY HEART

Let the words of my mouth, and the meditation of my heart, be acceptable in thy sight, O Lord, my strength, and my redeemer.   PSALMS 19:14

Meditation is an experience, and inasmuch as this experience is an individual one, it can never be confined within the limits of any predetermined pattern. Meditate; pray; dwell in the secret place of the most High in quietness and in peace; and you will discover that the truth you are seeking already abides within you.

Christ, the great light, is within you. Christ is the healer; Christ is the multiplier of loaves and fishes; Christ is that which supports, maintains, and sustains; but It is already within you. You will never find health, supply, or companionship by searching for them. These are embodied within you and they will unfold from your within-ness, as you learn to commune with the Father. You can draw on your Christhood for anything, and it will flow out from you to the extent of your realization of this truth. You are self-complete in God. Christ is your true identity, and in Christ, you are fulfilled in all your completeness. In this self-completeness in God, there is only one thing for which to pray; there is only one thing needful—spiritual illumination. Knock, and the door will be opened to you. Ask for spiritual illumination, for the gift of the Spirit, and God will reveal Itself as fulfillment.

In moments of uplifted consciousness, the ensuing meditations unfolded from within, revealing the gifts of the Spirit. These meditations follow no established or prescribed pattern, but each one is an expression of the spiritual impulse flowing into form. They are not to be followed slavishly nor are they to be used as a formula. Their only purpose is to serve as an inspiration, so that you may glimpse the beauty and joy of this experience and be encouraged to undertake the discipline required to discover the unplumbed depths of your own within-ness and, in so doing, launch forth into deeper and ever deeper experiences of awareness.

Meditation is a continuous song of gratitude that God is love, that God is here, and that God is now. It is resting in God's bosom, holding God's hand, and feeling the divine Presence. Rest in the contemplation of the Father's love and the Father's presence. Then you will be able to say: "My meditation of him shall be sweet: I will be glad in the Lord."

CHAPTER VI

THE EARTH IS THE LORD'S

The earth is the Lord's, and the fullness thereof; the world, and they that dwell therein.   PSALMS 24:1

When I consider thy heavens, the work of thy fingers, the moon and the stars, which thou hast ordained;

What is man that thou art mindful of him? and the son of man, that thou visitest him?

For thou hast made him a little lower than the angels, and hast crowned him with glory and honour.

Thou madest him to have dominion over the works of thy hands; thou hast put all things under his feet.   PSALMS 8:3-6

In the contemplation of God's universe, the mind is centered in God. As we quietly, gently, and peacefully observe God in action on earth as It is in heaven, we are witnessing the glory of God. Practicing this form of meditation or contemplation, day in and day out, will bring us to a state of consciousness where discursive thought slows down and finally stops. One of these days, as we are engaged in this spiritual activity of watching God at work, a second of silence will occur in which there is no thought of any kind. In that split second, the activity or presence of God will make Itself known to us. From that moment on, we know that God is closer than breathing, nearer than hands and feet, and that the kingdom of God is within us. Out of the void and darkness, out of the stillness of our consciousness, the Spirit of God moves to create for us our world of form:

I have come to this quiet hour to contemplate God and the things of God. Every blessing upon this earth is an emanation or an expression of God and God's law: the sun that warms us and the rain that feeds our plants and trees. The stars, the tides, and the moon all fulfill functions of God and yet appear as blessings to man. It could have been no accident that God hung the sun up in the sky, millions of miles away from the earth, just far enough away to give us the proper amount of warmth and the right amount of coolness. God really is the intelligence of this universe— an intelligence full of love and wisdom. The sun, the moon, and the stars move in their respective orbits according to a divine plan that makes the moon and stars visible at night and gives us the light of the sun by day.

God is the source of all that is. God's love is made evident in the fact that before man appeared on earth, everything was here necessary for his development, for his growth, and for his welfare. Even the minerals in the earth were given for man's use. The processes of nature that formed the iron, the oil, the gold, the uranium—all of these processes are of God. God must have known millions of years ago that these minerals would be necessary in the present age of industrialization and automation, because that long ago they were taking form in the ground. Millions of years ago God must have foreseen the billions of people who would inhabit the earth, because He created fertile ground, on which would grow trees, and shrubs, flowers, fruits, and vegetables:

And God said, let the earth bring forth grass, the herb yielding seed, and the fruit tree yielding fruit after his kind, whose seed is in itself, upon the earth.

God filled the oceans with fish and with elements not yet extracted from the sea which may someday support entire nations:

Let the waters bring forth abundantly the moving creature that hath life.
And God blessed them, saying, Be fruitful, and multiply, and fill the waters in the seas . . .

All of this is God's gift to man.

This gift is grace, God giving Itself to me. That grace is my sufficiency in all things: the grace that created galaxies of stars, a solar system of sun, moon, and planets; that filled the mountains with trees; the valleys with crops; the waters with fish; the air with birds. All this good, planted in the earth even before the need for it was apparent, is the evidence of God's grace. The divine Love and Wisdom which has provided for every need of this earth is my sufficiency. Can I ask for more than to know that the Intelligence that governs this universe is governing my individual affairs? Should I ask for more than the realization that the love shown forth in the creation and the maintenance of this universe is governing my life, my world, my business, and my home? Thy grace is sufficient to fill the earth; it is sufficient for my every need.

I behold God in all things and, especially, do I behold God in Its law and in Its love. God loves the fish in the sea and provides for their food and for their propagation. God loves the birds in the air and cares for them. God provides the gentle breezes and the cooling waters. God loves me, and has evidenced that love by incarnating Its own being, Its own life, Its own wisdom, and Its own love as me. I need only to obey the law—the law of one power and the law of love—and then all these things will be added. They are God's gift, without price. The things of God are mine, given freely in the measure of my acknowledgment of God as their source. God is the great giver of the universe, the great giver of Itself to this universe, giving Its love, intelligence, wisdom, direction, and strength to all.

As we contemplate the glories of God that already exist, we are acknowledging God and bearing witness to Its grace, which has provided all this good without our having asked for it, begged for it, or petitioned for it. We become witnesses of the activity of God on earth.

At night, looking up at the starry sky, no one is ever anxious about tomorrow's sun. Not one of us will sit up tonight to pray that the sun will rise tomorrow. God requires no supplication, information, or advice from us in regard to the government of Its universe, and even should we pray all night in an attempt to change the hour of sunrise, there is **no doubt but that the sun** will rise tomorrow at its appointed time. Tomorrow night the moon and the stars will continue to move in their orbits; the tides will rise and ebb twice in every twenty-four hours. Praying to God, petitioning God, or begging God will not change God's law. God's work is done; God's law is in operation.

In the contemplation of the wonders of God's universe, we transcend the desire to inform God of anything or to ask God for anything. Such contemplation lifts us to the heights of the Psalmist's vision that the earth is the Lord's and the fullness thereof. In a quiet, silent walk in a park, by seashore, lake, or river, in our aloneness, we catch that vision. We look up to the hills, to the mountains, to the heights of consciousness, and behold only that which God beholds and know only that which God knows. Anything that lifts us in consciousness above the clamor of the senses and the noises of this world will serve to bring us into the presence of God. When we reach the divine heights of inspiration, we find God. God is a deep silence; God is a stillness, the stillness of all that is human.

> Aloneness has been granted me.
> Whether on Bishop Street at noon,
> Or Kalakaua;
> On Waikiki at sunset,
> On the sands at Kailua

Before dawn,
I am alone.
I walk alone in crowds
And feel the solitary Self
In the moonlight on the beach.

Aloneness has been granted me.
To walk with men,
To fly the skies,
And sail the seas,
Wherever heart is raised to Him—
I walk alone.
At heat of day,
Or cool of eve,
On shore or city street,
The yearning Soul receives my Aloneness.

The sick are healed;
The restless are forgiven.
Alone, yet in the hearts
Of those who long for peace,
The restless feel my Aloneness;
The hungry eat it;
The thirsty drink it;
It washes the impure minds
Of those who do not know,
Touching the mind with Light.

Aloneness has been granted me,
Alone I sit behind the prison wall;
Alone I pace the sickroom floor;
Whatever danger threatens,
My aloneness breaks the spell,
Where misery craves company,
My Aloneness they may share.

Alone, I wake, and walk, and sleep—
Alone, I sit or stand.
Alone, I travel sea and sky
Alone, I walk and talk with men

Or stroll along the shady lane.
Aloneness has been granted me
Wherever I may be.

When through spiritual insight, we see through the appearance, all that we behold in this world is showing forth God's glory, God's work, God's law, and God's love for His children. The heavens and the earth were made for us; we were given dominion over them: "Thou madest him to have dominion over the works of thy hands; thou hast put all things under his feet . . ." We are God's greatest creation: God, the Soul of this universe, is manifesting Itself and sending Itself forth into individual expression as you and as me.

CHAPTER VII

FOR GOD SO LOVED THE WORLD

For God so loved the world, that he gave his only begotten Son, that whosoever believeth in him should not perish but have everlasting life.   JOHN 3:16

Behold, what manner of love the Father hath bestowed upon us, that we should be called the sons of God. . . . I JOHN 3:1

The secret of the beauty and glory of holiness is God manifest, God incarnate in the flesh. God so loved the world that He gave Himself to this world, appearing visibly as the Son of God, which, according to His promise, I am and which you are. God is my being and God is your being: God is our true identity.

Spiritually understood, this earth is heaven. Heaven and earth are one, because God has manifested Himself upon the earth. God has given unto Himself this universe made up of the stars, sun, moon, and planets. God has created for His glory this footstool which we call the earth. All this God has evolved from within Himself, and for His glory. God, in His own great glory, is manifested as individual being. We are not separate and apart from God, but we are the very essence of God, the very selfhood of God, unfolded, revealed, and brought into active expression as individual being.

All things in heaven and on earth are given unto us because of this relationship of divine sonship. All things that exist, exist for our purpose. As joint heirs with Christ in God, this earth is ours. From everlasting to everlasting we are fulfilled. God has ordained the law governing the union of Himself with His beloved Son, providing him with all that belongs to the Father, and drawing unto the Son all that the Father has established for him, since before the foundation of the world:

"I am come that they might have life, and that they might have it more abundantly." I am come that you might have life—My life—My life, your individual life. My life is the life of individual being, knowing no age, knowing no change, knowing no deterioration from its God-estate. But you must live and move and have your being in this consciousness of our oneness. I will never leave you nor forsake you, but you must abide in My Word, and you must let My Word abide in you. You must look unto Me and be saved.

There is a glory of the Father prepared for the Son. There is a peace—*My* peace—the peace that passeth understanding. This peace is embodied in the Soul of man: it is never dependent upon any external condition; it exists as the gift of God in the midst of us. Our mistake has been in seeking peace from each other, in believing that others had the power to give or to withhold peace, or in relying upon others for our harmony. In this reliance on people and outer circumstances has been our failure and the failure of the world. Only in God can peace be found. God has given to each one of us His infinite peace, His everlasting dominion, and His all-encompassing love.

God has not given us the spirit of fear, but of power, of love, and of a sound mind, because God is the very mind of our being. We have no mind apart from God. Our ignorance, our fear, and our insanity have been in the belief of a mind apart from God, the belief of a soul apart from God, a soul that could sin. God's Being is individual being, and when seen through spiritual vision, only the qualities of God and the nature of God comprise individual being.

"I and my Father are one . . . he that seeth me seeth him that sent me. . . . I am in the Father, and the Father in me." Spiritual discernment reveals God as the Father and God as the Son. In the realization of this oneness is our completeness and our perfection. There can be no peace, security, or joy separate and apart from God. Peace, security, and joy are inherent in God and for this reason must be indigenous to us through the realization of God as our own being.

The great secret of scripture is: in the beginning—God. In the beginning all that was, was God: now and forever, all that is, is God. God is appearing as the infinity, glory, and strength of Its own Being. It is not your being or my being, but Its infinite Being which appears outwardly as your being and as mine—I in *Him* and *He* in me, and this one Being spiritual, infinite, perfect, harmonious, whole, and complete. His Being is perfect; His understanding is infinite. His strength enables us to mount up as the eagle. His joy overflows our cup. Let us acknowledge His joy, His health, His understanding, His peace, His harmony, His purity, and His integrity. Let us drop "my" this or "my" that and "your" this or "your" that. His Being, expressing, as grace, is our sufficiency in all things. His grace—His presence, His joy, His love, His allness—is our sufficiency.

His love flows out as our love, but let us not claim it as your love or as mine. This love is flowing as the sun is shining, freely upon all. The sun shines without favoritism, never questioning the merits or worth of the recipients of its warmth and light. The sun shines; God loves. God's love flows freely to the just and the unjust, to the deserving and the undeserving, to the saint and the sinner alike. God's love pours into this universe, giving life to the seed, strength to the growing plants, protection to animal, vegetable, and mineral life. God's love is the supporting and animating influence of all creation, because all creation is Love, Itself, freely flowing.

All that is, is in and of God. There are no exceptions. There must be no labels of criticism or of judgment or of condemnation. Above all things we must not judge after the testimony of the eyes or the ears. God is too pure to see iniquity, and when we recognize our true identity as God in expression, we shall see as God sees. As we behold ourselves spiritually endowed, we become beholders of God appearing in all and through all. But we can do this only as we relinquish those judgments that come to us by the seeing of the eye and the hearing of the ear.

His infinite understanding becomes our understanding. His infinite love becomes our love. God's blessings are not ours because you are you or I am I. They are God's blessings unto God—God's blessings flowing unto Its own Self as the Son, the Father bestowing His all as the Son. It is the Father giving, the Son receiving, and yet one, only one—Father and Son. In oneness, in conscious union with God is our strength; in conscious union with God is our supply; in conscious union with God is our peace, joy, power, dominion, and our every blessing.

If God is the infinite nature of our being, what need is there to be envious, to be jealous, to be hateful, or to be ambitious? When we know that God is the source of our inner satisfaction, how can we long for anything external to our own being? In this relationship, the blessings of God unfold as our experience.

Our Father has imparted to us Himself. In the realization of our true identity, we partake of the very Body of God: that is eating the Body and drinking the Blood. " 'I have meat to eat that ye know not of.' I can give you life—waters that spring into life eternal—the invisible waters, invisible wine, invisible meat." This is partaking of the living God, or the living Word, and watching the Word become flesh and dwell among us—God incarnate in the flesh.

CHAPTER VIII

YE ARE THE TEMPLE

Know ye not that ye are the temple of God . . . that your body is the temple . . . of the living God." I CORINTHIANS 16:19

The body is the temple of the living God, a temple not made with hands, not mortally conceived, but eternal in the heavens; that is, eternal in time and space; eternal in life; eternal in spirit, in soul, and in substance. God made all that was made, and all that God made was made *of God*, partaking of the very nature of God which is eternality, immortality, and perfection. God made the body in Its own image and likeness.

God is life. An activity of God, operating in a seed, brings forth a child with all the potentialities of adulthood embodied in one tiny little form—not merely a piece of matter, but an intelligence and a soul accompanying that body. The Spirit of God does this, but, in his vanity, man has arrogated to himself the role of a creator. Men and women have assumed that because they were fathers and mothers they were originators, instead of knowing that they are the instruments through which God acts to express Himself—not to perpetuate you or me, or my children or your children. God operates as love in our consciousness to

75

produce His own image and likeness. This expression of God we have called your child and mine, forgetting that this is *God's* child, and not a personal creation or a personal possession. We pray to God to maintain and sustain our children; but they are not *our* children: they are *God's* children. It is not necessary to pray that God maintain and sustain His own children. It is God's prerogative to create, maintain, and sustain Its own image and likeness.

God is the creator of all that is. God, then, is the creator of man's body. "Know ye not that your body is the temple of the living God?" We call this body your body and my body, but it is not ours. It is God's body, formed by Him for His pleasure, made in His image and likeness, governed by His law, and created to show forth His glory.

On our Christmas trees there are lights of all colors— red, blue, purple. Electricity transmits its light through these multicolored bulbs of all shapes and sizes. The bulbs, in and of themselves, are not the source of the light; they are merely the instruments through which the light shines. So it is that when we see human, animal, or plant life, we mistake their visible form for the life which animates and is the substance of that form. God is the life and the substance of all form, the creative principle of all that is. God is the activity governing the functions and organs of the body. It is God that animates all men and women. God is the wisdom, the integrity, and the purity of the Soul of man. God is the strength of man.

Let us not be deceived by appearances, not even by good appearances. Let us not call one person strong and another one beautiful. We must look behind the appearance to the invisible Life which makes all this beauty of form possible. Then we can enjoy every aspect of creation, every appearance, whether it is the human body, an animal species, or a plant. These are forms of life, but if we do not understand that Life which vitalizes these forms, they may appear as either good or bad, young or old, sick or well, rich or poor.

A limited human sense of life relies on shifting values and invests the forms life assumes with power for good or evil; a spiritual sense of life, however, enjoys the form while recognizing the Infinite Invisible as the essence of that form. If we take our eyes away from the form long enough to look behind it into the Invisible and see God as the principle of all life, we shall understand the difference between material living and spiritual living. The truth entertained in our consciousness is the law of life, of harmony, and of resurrection unto our body.

God made this form, my infinite divine form, to show forth my true identity. My body is a manifestation, the image of the I that I am. My body is an expression of life showing forth all that I am, because my body is the I that I am formed, and formed spiritually, eternally, and immortally. I am true identity—eternal identity—and my body is the temple, the instrument of my activity and of my living.

As against this spiritual truth, there is that form which I see in a mirror; there are the expressions of nature, such as trees, flowers, vegetables, and fruits. These are not spiritual being or body: these are the concepts that are entertained humanly of being and body.

If I look in a mirror, I may see myself as young or old, sick or well, stout or thin, but I am not seeing myself at all: I am seeing my body. That is my body, but I am invisible. Even this body which I see with my eyes is but a limited, finite concept of the body. That is the reason the body appears to keep changing. In reality, the body never changes; only the concept which I entertain about body changes.

Who am I? What am I? Where am I? Let us look down at our feet and ask ourselves: Is this I? Are these feet I or are they mine? Am I in the feet or do I possess these feet? Let us travel on up to the knee. Am I in the legs or are these legs mine? If they are injured, am I hurt; or is it my legs that are injured? Is there not an I, an identity which is not the legs? Let us go on up to the waist, to the chest, the neck, and finally the head. Am I in any of these or are these parts of the body mine? Is there not an I separate and apart from the body, an I which possesses the body? The body is an instrument for my activity, my movement, as much mine as is my automobile. Am I in the ears, eyes, mouth, tongue, throat, or are they mine? Am I in this body; am I this body; or is this body mine? Is it not a temple, an instrument given to me for my use?

Look at my hands. Can they of themselves give or withhold, or must I give or withhold using the hands as an instrument in either case? Can my hands be generous or miserly? Have my hands the power to give or the power to withhold; or does all that power reside in me? Is there not something called "I" that gives through these hands or that may sometimes withhold through these same hands? Can the hands move up or down, left or right? Does the heart give me permission to live or does life animate the heart? If my hands cannot give and cannot withhold, how then can my heart give life or withhold life? If my hands are not self-acting, how can my heart, liver, lungs, or kidneys be self-acting? As material organs, can my eyes see or my ears hear? Can the organs of this body move of their own accord? Is there not something called "I" which functions through this body? Is there not something called "I" which walks the street through these legs or by means of these legs? Is there not an "I" which functions through the instrumentality of this body?

I am being; my being is not dependent upon body: my body is dependent upon my being. The I that I am governs my body. My body has no will of its own, no intelligence of its own, no action of its own. My body responds to me; it is governed by me. My body is the image and likeness of me; my body is the manifestation of me, the I that I am. There is a Spirit in me: the breath of the Almighty giveth me life. The activity of God in me governs my bodily functions, organs, and muscles. An invisible Spirit acts upon every organ and function of my body to maintain it and sustain it unto eternity. Nothing from without, to defile or make a lie, can enter this temple of the living God. Whatever is of God, God will maintain and sustain. Whatever is a mortal concept of my body may pass from sight, but the truth about my body will live forever because my body is the temple of the living God.

All power is in God functioning as the law of my body. God is the only law, just as God is the only lawgiver. All law, therefore, is spiritual, and my body is governed by spiritual law. Spiritual law does not overcome or nullify material law, but spiritual law reveals that the material sense of law is of no effect. "Stand still, and see the salvation of the Lord . . . not by might, nor by power, but by my spirit." This body is the temple of God. I need not struggle; I need not seek healing. The battle is not mine, but God's, and rightly understood, it is not a battle. It is a revelation that this body is the temple of the living God and is governed by spiritual law. Every mortal or material concept which I have entertained about the body dissolves in the recognition that my body is the temple of the living God, ageless, timeless, diseaseless, deathless. God is the central theme of my being; God is the central theme of my body.

God is the substance and strength of my body. "I can do all things through Christ which strengtheneth me. . . . The Lord is my strength and song. . . . God is my strength and power: and he maketh my way perfect. . . . the Lord is the strength of my life; of whom shall I be afraid?" If I look to my body for strength, I find disease, death, and weakness. If I agree that Christ is my strength, that my divine sonship is my strength, that the word of God in the midst of me is my strength, my youth, my vitality, my all in all, I find life eternal.

"I am the bread of life: he that cometh to me shall never hunger; and he that believeth on me shall never thirst."

I *have water. If you ask of Me, I can give you water, a water that springs up into life eternal. I do not live by bread alone. Every Word of God that comes to my consciousness is bread, wine, water, and meat to my Soul, my spirit, my being, and my body. Every Word of truth that I permit to fill my consciousness is the meat the world knows not of. Every Word of truth I maintain in consciousness is a wellspring of water, springing up into life everlasting.*

When I am empty of the Word of God, I am empty of sustenance. The most palatable food is like so much sawdust —mere bulk in my system—unless the Word of God accompanies it to act as a law of digestion, assimilation, and elimination.

I am the wine, the inspiration, the spiritual wisdom. I am that which enlightens and uplifts. God it is that enlightens and uplifts; God it is that inspires; God it is that illumines. I can know all things through Christ which is my wisdom: the Son of God in me is my wisdom. The Word of God in me is bread, wine, water. The world knoweth it not; I keep it hidden secretly within me, because if the world knew, it would not understand. The Word of God in the midst of me is mighty, revealing the perfect temple of God—my body, the body not made with hands, eternal in the heavens.

In this type of meditation, we drop all form and go beyond the visible to the Invisible. Then, we shall behold the Invisible upholding the visible. We must live and move and have our being in God-consciousness. Let us live, dwell in the secret place of the most High. Then we shall see the body as it really is: the temple not made with hands eternal in the heavens. "Behold the tabernacle of God is with men, and he will dwell with them. . . . and there shall in no wise enter into it anything that defileth, neither whatsoever worketh abomination, or maketh a lie."

CHAPTER IX

THE SILVER IS MINE

The silver is mine, and the gold is mine, saith the Lord of hosts.

The glory of this latter house shall be greater than of the former, saith the Lord of hosts.   HAGGAI 2:8, 9

Except the Lord build the house, they labour in vain that build it.   PSALMS 127:1

"Except the Lord build the house," unless God is understood to be the source of our supply, there is no permanent supply. This "house" is our individual consciousness. When this consciousness is unenlightened human consciousness, it is barren; it lacks the spiritual substance from which supply flows.

"Ye have sown much, and bring in little; ye eat, but ye have not enough; ye drink, but ye are not filled with drink; ye clothe you, but there is none warm; and he that earneth wages earneth wages to put it into a bag with holes." All this is true of you—"ye," the unenlightened consciousness. As human beings, we all have sown much and reaped little; we have worked hard and many times accomplished nothing; we have earned wages and often have had nothing left,

because all this came from an unenriched, barren consciousness. Out of the barrenness of human consciousness, regardless of what we build, our efforts are not permanent or
lasting. We eat, and hunger again; we drink, and thirst
again; we engage in all the activities of human life, but
nothing endures. "It is vain . . . to rise up early, to sit up
late" trying to demonstrate supply.

Then we are told: "Thus saith the Lord of hosts; Consider
your ways." With this admonition, comes the instruction
to go up to the mountain: to go up into a high state of
consciousness; to go into the high places, and from there
"bring wood, and build the house." Every time we meditate
or fill ourselves with "the meat ye know not of" or the
water of life or the wine of life, or the bread of life, meaning
spiritual substance and food, we are building the house of
spiritual consciousness, a consciousness of truth.

When that house has been built, the Lord says, "I will
take pleasure in it, and I will be glorified." Now we speak of *I*:

Yet now be strong, O Zerubbabel, saith the Lord; and be
strong, O Joshua, son of Josedech, the high priest; and be
strong, all ye people of the land, saith the Lord, and work: for
I am with you, saith the Lord of hosts:

. . . . . .

For thus saith the Lord of hosts; Yet once, it is a little while,
and I will shake the heavens, and the earth, and the sea, and
the dry land;
And I will shake all nations, and the desire of all nations
shall come: and I will fill this house with glory, saith the Lord
of hosts.
The silver is mine, and the gold is mine, saith the Lord of
hosts:
The glory of this latter house shall be greater than of the
former, saith the Lord of hosts: and in this place will I give
peace, saith the Lord of hosts.

—HAGGAI 2:4, 6-9

Before this, it was all "ye"; it was ours, and no matter how much of it we had, it came to little. Now let us turn and acknowledge that the silver is the Lord's and the power is the Lord's. Let us begin to understand that the earth is the Lord's and the fullness thereof. The *I*, within us, is multiplying out of the unseen resources of Spirit—not taking anything from anyone, not dividing that which is already in the world, and not drawing upon the visible resources of the earth. Now supply is multiplied from within us. Now we are drawing forth from the invisible storehouse of our own being. Our individual consciousness is the storehouse of infinite spiritual unfoldment. The moment we begin to draw from this inexhaustible storehouse, which never takes account of what is in the visible world, we cease being concerned with how much or how little we have, or with whether the current economic status of the world be one of prosperity or depression. God has given to us infinite bounty, and it is unlimited in its expression, as long as we recognize that the earth is the Lord's; the silver is the Lord's; and the gold is the Lord's. It is only when we are trying to get our share of the world's goods, believing that the earth, the silver, and the gold are personal possessions, belonging to human beings, that we are limited. A sense of finiteness creeps in, and regardless of the number and amount of personal possessions acquired, there is often nothing left over. In the realization that the silver is Mine and the gold is Mine, we draw on such an infinite source that the more we use the more remains. When we have God, we have the infinity of supply.

We experience lack or we are supplied according to our state of consciousness. Whatever is to appear in our life must appear as the result of the activity of truth in our consciousness. If we maintain the same consciousness tomorrow that we have today, we cannot expect any different results tomorrow. To enjoy a more satisfying experience tomorrow, there must be an expanding activity of truth in our consciousness today.

As we begin to understand that God is our individual consciousness, and that God is infinite, we perceive the true nature of supply as that which is invisible; we no longer judge by appearances as to the amount of our supply, nor do we ever come to that place where there is an absence of supply. Never can an individual with a consciousness of supply lack the forms of supply. During wars or sudden depression, or during a period of stress and strain, such as the Hebrews experienced on their journey from Egypt to the Promised Land, there may be a temporary absence of the forms of supply. But with the wisdom that supply is the Infinite Invisible appearing as form, "the years of the locust" are quickly restored, and supply is revealed as omnipresent and abundant.

We can draw on our Christhood for anything, anything at all, to the extent of our realization of this truth. There may be a multitude clamoring to be fed and no storehouse or barn from which to draw food—only a few loaves and fishes. How can they be fed? As human beings, there is no alternative except starvation; but as Christ-being, we turn to the Father within, and draw forth from the depths of the infinity of our own being an abundance of supply, of food, or whatever is necessary. Out of our Christhood, the infinite nature of our being, can flow millions of words, millions of ideas, and why not millions of dollars. What is the difference? The source is the same; the substance is the same: in the beginning was God, and God was Spirit; everything that comes forth comes from the Father, from Spirit.

God is; infinity is; infinite good already is. Infinite abundance is filling all space, awaiting only my recognition. All that is necessary for my unfoldment is this very moment established in my consciousness. The invisible Soul of me is the substance of all form.

*Never again can I be dependent upon any person; never
again can I be at the mercy of my own strength or financial
resources. There is Something beyond my own wisdom
and my own power. There is a support, that upon which I
can lean in complete faith and trust and from which I receive whatever is necessary for my fulfillment. The presence
of that Spirit in me appears as water, when I need it,
or as bread. That Spirit is the substance of whatever is to
be made manifest; it is an invisible law operating as a law
of multiplication and as a law of attraction. I relax in
confidence and assurance into a pillow of the Christ.*

*"The silver is mine; the gold is mine." God is the eternal
storehouse of all good. I turn within to that infinite storehouse and let the good of God flow out into expression. I
care not in what form it flows, nor do I try to direct its
flow, because my heavenly Father knoweth what things I
have need of before I ask him. It is his good pleasure to
provide all good for me. I draw forth my supply from the
invisible storehouse within my own being; I, within me,
is multiplying out of the unseen resources of Spirit. God is
infinite being and infinite in expression, pouring through
me as unlimited supply.*

*Good is here and now where I am. I do not live on yes-
terday's manna. Yesterday's lack or yesterday's abundance
of manna does not determine the amount of my supply
today. Neither do I live on tomorrow's manna. In the consciousness of God's ever-presence, there are no tomorrows;
time and space are not; there is only the eternal now and
the holy ground of God's infinity. In this moment and in
this place, the manna falls abundantly. All good flows out
from the center of my being supplying my every need, filling
me with the living water, the bread of life, and the meat
which perisheth not.*

It is necessary to eat and drink of this truth, to digest
and assimilate it, and to make it a part of our very being,
until a day, a week, a month, or a year from now, we begin

to see the fruitage of it, in the lessening of doubt and the measure of peace that is established within.

Life becomes entirely different once we have caught the vision of the great truth that the Word, which proceedeth out of the mouth of God, is the substance of our life, our water, our wine, our bread, and our meat. We begin to see that that which is outward and tangible is but the effect of that which is invisible. We shall never again judge our supply by how many dollars we possess, but by how much of God we realize. "The silver is mine, and the gold is mine. . . . In thy presence is fullness of life," and therefore we turn within to gain an awareness of that Presence.

CHAPTER X

THE PLACE WHEREON
THOU STANDEST

The place whereon thou standest is holy ground. Exodus 3:5

For since the beginning of the world men have not heard, nor perceived by the ear, neither hath the eye seen, O God, beside thee, what he hath prepared for him that waiteth for him.   Isaiah 64:4

Thou wilt shew me the path of life: in thy presence is fullness of joy; at thy right hand there are pleasures for evermore.
                                                    Psalms 16:11

Wherever we are at this moment is holy ground. In this awareness, we can relax and let the Father reveal Its plan for us. God, the Father, is infinite, and that infinity manifests itself through us as our activity, whether it be that of a minister, physician, lawyer, nurse, teacher, healer, housewife, businessman, or mechanic. The work assigned to us today may not be of our choosing; but if, instead of kicking against the pricks, we remember that God is working out Its plan on earth, and that we are here only to show forth the glory of the Father, there will be nothing limited, confined, or finite about our life or our activity.

87

The Father, being infinite, manifests Itself infinitely.

We have no right to interfere with the divine plan; our responsibility is to begin where we are, confident that the place whereon we stand is holy ground. That place may be a prison, a hospital, or a position of high honor; but however high or lowly, that place is holy ground. There we play the part assigned to us. There we remain, until God moves us. We interfere with the divine plan when we let the little "I" decide where it should function, instead of being satisfied to let the Christ determine our activity.

Nothing will bring forth such an abundant sense of life as the realization of our self-completeness in God, not self-completeness in Jane, Jim, or Joel, but self-completeness in God. This self-completeness in God is made manifest as the harmony and abundance of Jane, Jim, or Joel, but it still is not their personal achievement of abundance, success, intelligence, or love. The wisdom of the Father manifests and expresses through every person who permits it to operate in his experience by recognizing his oneness with the Father. It is not too difficult to be what the world calls a go-getter, attaining an important and influential position, and thereby, glorify and magnify the personal sense of I. It is much more difficult to wait for the world to come to us; but if we once realize that the Christ is the real mind of our being, the real soul, the real wisdom, the real love, we shall find that everything and everybody will gravitate to that Christ, and our divine activity will be brought to our very door.

If, however, in our egotism, we believe that our success is dependent upon, or is the result of, our personal efforts and qualities, we may find that success empty and fleeting. "Ye looked for much, and, lo, it came to little; and when ye brought it home, I did blow upon it. Why? saith the Lord of hosts. Because of mine house that is waste, and ye run every man unto his own house"—to his own intellect, his own sense of wisdom, his own spirituality, instead of to God, the Infinite Invisible, the source and fount of his being.

In going within, we do not turn to our own spirituality or our own goodness or our own strength or our own knowledge; but we go within to unleash the Infinite Invisible. The only permanence is in that completeness which comes through God, through the realization of the spiritual nature of our being, and the ability to let it manifest and express itself in whatever direction it may take.

In this stillness, as we touch this vision of our oneness with the Father, God pours Its infinite good through us. We shall find that, without any strain or struggle, leaves will unfold, little buds will bloom, and by standing still, active in the work that is given us to do each day, the fruitage will follow. Each one of us has some kind of work to do today. If we do that work today, without concern for tomorrow, in the realization that God, through the invisible Christ of our being, is ever pouring Its essence, substance, and bounty into us, the next day something else is given us to do.

Tomorrow there may be another mission, another work, or another activity for us. Nothing can keep our work from us. When the Christ has been realized, Its activity can never be impaired, impeded, delayed, or hindered. God has a way of wiping away every obstruction. Nothing can prevent the fruitage from appearing in our life when its time has come. When that moment comes, the God-force will thrust it into expression, just as inexorably as the unborn child is expelled from the womb, when its moment arrives to appear on the scene.

The government is on His shoulder. As we listen to that *I* that is deep within our own being, we are led of the Spirit. We behold the hand of God reaching right up through us, in us, coming out into manifestation and placing Its glory in our experience as our activity. We witness the hand of God within us as it offers up its good; our good coming to us from within us, not from without, but from the kingdom of God which is within us; not from man whose breath is in his nostrils, not from man who would give or withhold, or who could give or withhold. The hand of God does not withhold; the hand of God does not limit.

Step by step, the infinite Christ leads us from one activity to another. It may lead us from the business world to the world of music, or from a world of family duties to the ministry of healing or teaching. The Christ can make of us anything It chooses. It has no favorite occupation; no occupation is more spiritual than another so long as it is of a constructive nature. All are equal in the sight of God; all are the activity of grace appearing in infinite form and variety.

Life by grace is lived with the understanding that tomorrow is not our concern but God's concern. The grace of God does not bestow partial success or happiness, nor does it demand that which cannot be fulfilled. God brings the task to us, but grace also provides the understanding, the strength, and the wisdom to perform it. Whatever is necessary for the fulfillment of that task, whether it be transportation, funds, books, people, teachers, or teaching, is always forthcoming. Everything that comes by grace comes as fulfillment.

Because we have more, more is expected of us. We can fulfill any and every demand made upon us if we realize that the demand is not made upon us, but upon Him that sent us. "I can of mine own self do nothing," but the Father within is equal to every demand. Divine grace enables us to perform everything necessary and, in its own time, frees us of undue burdens through the realization that God shoulders them. When God meets an obligation He has a way of meeting it forever, so that it is not a recurring or a continuing one.

Let us pour out our gifts of the Spirit to the multitudes; but let us never seek the multitudes. We do not go up and down the highways and byways, even of our family, trying to find somebody upon whom to force this gift; because if we squander the gift of the Spirit on the unprepared thought, we shall find ourselves depleted. We wait for the multitudes to come to us. Should the multitude consist of only one person, we wait for that one to come to us. We sit quietly at home, or in our shop or office, with our finger on our lips, keeping our treasure hidden from the world. Those who are receptive respond to the light within us, and recognize the glint in our eyes, or the smile on our face. As they come, one by one, let us accept each one as the multitude. They come to us for bread, which we give to them, and cold water and warm water, too. We give them what they are seeking. We give it to them gently; we give it to them gradually; we give it to them with love, with joy, and with the power of authority. We can draw upon the infinity of our being, and anything will flow: words of truth, compassion, love, healing, grace, finances, food, water, drink, protection, care, companionship—all these will flow forth from the Christ within us.

Let us be reborn in the spiritual awareness of the infinite nature of our own being and our already Self-completeness. Let our prayer be:

Thank you, Father; I am. That which I have been seeking, I already am. All is embodied within my own being, and it is only necessary for me to let it flow into manifestation. Nothing can be added to me; nothing can be taken from me.

"I can do all things through Christ which strengtheneth me. . . . I live; yet not I"; it is really God living in me and as me. God performs those things which are given me to do. I am that center of God-being through which God pours Its infinite good to this universe; God uses me as Its instrument. My only purpose on earth is to bear witness to God's glory, to God's greatness, and to God's infinity: to show forth God's handiwork.

God is my parent; God is my environment; and God is my inheritance. This I that I am is not limited by any personal sense of consciousness, subconsciousness, or superconscious-

ness. It is limited only to whatever limitations are imposed upon God, and since God is infinite, there are no limitations. All that the universal consciousness is, is pouring Itself into me. I let God flow into me, through me, and out into this vast world.

I am come that ye might be fulfilled. I go to prepare a place for you. I go: that I of my being, that divine Ego, prepares the way. My heavenly Father knoweth that I have need of these things, and it is his good pleasure to give them to me—not to make me struggle, not to make me strive, not to make me fight or labor, beg or plead for them. My good is mine by right of divine inheritance.

I awaken in the morning with confidence, rejoicing in whatever work is given me to do. Whatever that work is, I do it, not in order to earn a living or in the sense of performing an onerous duty; but, with joy and gladness, I let it unfold as the activity of God expressing through me.

As we continuously look to the Christ as the source and fount of our good, thus will it flow. As we place our complete reliance on the divine Presence within, we become that point through which God shines to the world; and we willingly accept our role as a channel, through which good finds an outlet to the world, instead of looking to the world, expecting that good to flow from it to us. All the Godhead pours out from us to those who do not yet know about their conscious oneness with God. Spiritual man rests in his conscious union with God and lets the infinity of good manifest: never does he seek, desire, or want; he stands and serves. The more of a transparency for the Christ we are, the more of a servant we become. We serve as an instrument through which the Father feeds His flock. We become the avenue through which the infinite spiritual good of the divine Source pours forth into visible expression.

CHAPTER XI

FOR LOVE IS OF GOD

Beloved, let us love one another: for love is of God. I John 4:7

That they all may be one; as thou, Father, art in me, and I in thee, that they also may be one in us . . . John 17:21

Living, moving, and having our being in continuous God-consciousness reveals the secret of living with other people. And what is the secret of our relationship to other people? How do we achieve harmony in our interpersonal relationships?

From a human standpoint, satisfactory relationships between groups of people and between individuals depend upon the quality of communication. All too frequently attempts at communication result in misunderstanding and "confusion worse confounded." Often these unhappy effects are due to the prevalent belief that there are many minds with diverse interests: that we can get something from somebody, or that somebody may take something from us.

The Infinite Way, however, approaches this problem from an entirely different point of view. Our secret lies in a new concept of human relations: It is a relationship based on oneness, springing from a conviction that we are not beings separate and apart from one another; but that our oneness with God constitutes our oneness with one another.

God is individual mind; the mind of God in me addresses the mind of God in you. The one infinite Intelligence, acting through me, communicates with the one infinite Intelligence acting through you. One Intelligence speaks; one Intelligence hears; we are one. We are in agreement, not because we agree with each other, but because God agrees with Itself. God is the only mind; so in this one mind there can be no misunderstandings. God speaks unto God. Life reveals itself unto Life. Soul speaks unto Soul. I am but an instrument through which infinite Intelligence and divine Love are being revealed to the infinite Intelligence and divine Love of those who come within range of my consciousness. In that flow of Love from you to me, and from me to you, there is no separation.

The pressures of the world not only would separate us from God, but they would separate man from man, man from wife, parent from child, friend from friend, employer from employee. The world has made us natural enemies of one another. One animal preys upon another, and the great animal, man, preys upon all the other animals. The way of the world is separation; the way of the Christ is oneness. Isaiah caught this vision of oneness when he said: "The wolf also shall dwell with the lamb, and the leopard shall lie down with the kid; and the calf and the young lion and the fatling together. . . . They shall not hurt nor destroy in all my holy mountain."

The essential ingredient of all satisfactory relationships is love. Our love for God is made manifest in our love for man. We are not only one with God, but we are one with the children of God: with our families and relatives; with our church members; with our business associates; with our friends. When we recognize God as our neighbor, we become members of the household of God, saints in the spiritual kingdom: there is a complete surrender of self into the infinite Sea of Spirit. The good of God flows to us through all who become a part of our universe. To those who live in communion with God, serving God through their fellow man, the promise is literally kept: All that I have is thine.

No longer is there a need or a desire for any person or any thing. Every *hing and every person become part of our being. What we surrender, we have; what we hold in the grasp of possession, we lose. Every thing we release, we draw to us; every thing we loose, we have; every thing we set free, we bind to us forever. "Loose him and let him go." Let everyone be loosed in Christ. We trust everyone to the God of his own being. We do not hold anyone in bondage to a debt of love, hate, fear, or doubt. We do not demand even love from anyone. We agree that no man owes us anything. Only when we do not feel a debt of obligation and only when we hold no one in a debt of obligation to us, are we free, and do we set our world free.

If we maintain our relationship of oneness with God, consciously realized, there will always be those in our experience who are instruments of God, sharing with us as we share with them, drawing on the same illimitable Oneness. If we expect love from one another, we obstruct and limit its flow to us. But if we maintain our conscious union with God, through a constant realization that I and the Father are one, then we open the way for the activity of God to flow to us, through anyone and everyone receptive and responsive to the God-impulse. Our contact with God is our contact with every person or place that can, in any way, play a part in the unfolding of our daily experience, including not only persons and places within range of our immediate environment, but throughout the universe. Wherever there is good for us in the world, it finds its way to us.

Our good comes through grace. This grace will appear as normal everyday avenues or channels, if we do not interfere with its operation by planning how it is to be expressed. Understanding God to be the giver of all good, we do not look to one another even for those things which constitute our human or our legal rights. In circumstances warranting court action, we naturally would take the necessary human steps to obtain competent legal counsel and to present our case in the best way possible. Our faith and trust, however, would not rest in the technicalities of legal procedure, but in God as the fount of all justice. The judge, jury, lawyers, and witnesses would be regarded as instruments expressing the justice of God.

The attitude of others toward us is strictly their own demonstration. If they act in accord with good, so it is to them; if their actions are contrary to good, the reaping of discord is likewise unto them. Only in proportion as we are looking to them for good is there the possibility of their doing evil to us. None can do good or evil to us, because we have submitted ourselves to the government and control of God. We look only to the Father within, and therefore the thoughts or deeds of man can never touch us. We are responsible only for our own conduct toward all, and that conduct must be in accord with the great command: love thy neighbor as thyself; love your enemies; forgive seventy times seven; pray for them which despitefully use you. Never fear or hate those who act contrary to the divine law of the one Self; but rejoice in those who let God use them as instruments for good.

We are faced with humanity at many levels, some good, some bad, and some intolerable. As humanity, mankind is graded, falling into varying states of consciousness. Living merely as human beings, with their inner resources untapped, unaware of their true identity, life for some becomes a hopeless struggle against insuperable odds—ill health, small earnings, and high taxes. To cloak their failure and sense of inadequacy, some people assume a bravado or affect an exuberance of outer joy to conceal their disappointment

and frustration. Yet these people, as do all people, hunger
for love. And how do they want to be loved? As we do,
first by being understood. Most of us are convinced that
no one understands us; if our friends and relatives really
understood us, they would forgive us more. Whenever we
come in contact with differing degrees of humanhood, our
attitude should be that of the Master: "Father, forgive
them; for they know not what they do"; they have not
been awakened to their Christhood. The measuring rod
always must be: regardless of the appearance, God is their
true being; God is the only law governing them; and their
only qualities are God-bestowed.

There is only One—only one infinite Being. There is only
one Person, since God is one and God is infinite. Just as
there is only one life, the God-life, permeating our garden,
even though that life may appear as twelve different species;
so it is, that even though our friends and acquaintances
may be numbered by the hundreds, there is only one life
manifested in individual expression. We can never fear
a person if we remember that God is one, that there is
only One, and that that one Being is God. In that oneness,
there can be no discord, inharmony, or injustice to anybody.

Our sense of forgiveness is a realization that no one can
harm us, because the grace of God maintains and sustains
our relationship of oneness with the Father, under any
and all circumstances. There is an invisible thread binding
us all together: that thread is the Christ. If we are bound
to one another by material ties of any nature, these ties
soon become burdensome. Whether the tie be one of mem-
bership in an organization, some form of human obligation,
or a tie of blood or marriage; as long as it is of a material
nature, it will irk. Only when the love behind these material
ties is so pure that it is devoid of all selfish consideration
will the relationship be satisfying, permanent, and mutually
beneficial.

There can be no real, enduring love in any relationship

into which God does not enter. There is no miracle of love in any marriage unless God is the foundation stone. If we know the love of God, we shall know the love of man. That love for God is a complete surrender in the mystical union of Father and Son: God, all that I have is Thine, just as all that Thou hast is mine. My time, my hands, my life are at Thy service. If men and women have experienced a complete surrender to God, if they have become one with God, then when the time comes for human marriage, they will enter into that same kind of a relationship with each other, and the words of the marriage ceremony will become a reality—the two become one.

Home is the expression of the consciousness of the individuals comprising the household. It takes on the atmosphere of the consciousness of those who make it. In a house, as such, there is neither love nor hate, sin nor purity, disease nor health; but if the members of that household permit their consciousness to be filled with thoughts of sin, disease, lack, limitation, suspicion, or fear; then discord, inharmony, and impoverishment will reign in that home. On the other hand, if the consciousness of those who make the home expresses love, understanding, faith, courage, hope, and assurance, home becomes a sanctuary. The vision of the new Jerusalem is built into that home—one holy city governed by love.

It is true that many of us cannot take our entire household with us into the kingdom of heaven. We may not succeed in making of our home that holy city, but we can resolve to remain steadfast in our realization of the Christ-identity of every person in our home—not outwardly voicing or preaching it in a multitude of meaningless words, but in silence maintaining our spiritual integrity, letting our life stand as a living testimony to the truth realized.

The Master made his demonstration for himself and for his followers in the silence of his own being. He did not hesitate to retire from the throngs pressing about him in order to have his days alone. We, too, can find our quiet periods of renewal, early in the morning, late at night, in the middle of the night, or at intervals during the day, by seizing brief respites from the demands of family life. Our realization of truth externalizes in the harmony and peace of our home. The Word is made flesh.

Unless, through these periods of silence, God enters into our relationship with our family, all our efforts and work to build home may come to naught. The material water, bread, or wine we may give the members of the family—the service—does not satisfy, and the next day they will hunger and thirst again. It is only in proportion to our recognition of our Christhood and the true identity of the members of our household that we are able to give the living waters: "Whosoever drinketh of the water that I shall give him shall never thirst." Then God fulfills Itself through us, as we fulfill our part, by bringing peace to individual consciousness.

When we are consciously aware of our union with God, turning to the Father within as the source of all good, our relationship with one another is pure and completely free of any desire to get, to have, or to possess anything or anyone which someone else has. A spiritual relationship is a giving one, a sharing one, and a co-operative one. It is like giving gifts to our children, to husbands, wives, brothers, sisters, or friends: not for any return; not for any reason; not because they have earned or deserved them; but just for the joy of expressing love. When our relationship to one another is based, not on what we deserve or have earned from one another, but on what lies within our hearts to give or share with one another—not only money, but all the courtesies of life: co-operation; forgiveness; understanding; mutuality; trust; and helpfulness—then, and then only, will that relationship be permanent, a pure gift of the Spirit, a pure offering of ourselves. "For love is of God."

CHAPTER XII

FOR HE IS THY LIFE

For I have no pleasure in the death of him that dieth, saith the Lord God: wherefore turn yourselves, and live ye.

EZEKIEL 18:32

. . . for He is thy life, and the length of thy days . . .

DEUTERONOMY 30:20

In my Father's house are many mansions: if it were not so, I would have told you.   JOHN 14:2

He that believeth on me hath everlasting life.   JOHN 6:47

And this is the will of him that sent me, that every one which seeth the Son and believeth on him, may have everlasting life. . . .   JOHN 6:40

Immortality is the realization of our true identity as God-being, an identity without beginning and without end, eternal and everlasting: It is a recognition of God as the Father and God as the Son. To those on the spiritual path, this is not a new idea. It is the foundation stone upon which rests every great spiritual teaching known to man. But the essence of this teaching has been buried in the prevalent concepts of immortality as a Methuselah-plus existence in this world, or as an eternal existence of bliss after death. The first is merely a gilded notion of longevity. The second is based upon the faulty premise that death is a part of God's creation, whereas the Master clearly stated, "The last enemy that shall be overcome is death."

It is true that, at some time or other, we all pass from human sight. Each, in his own time, will leave this plane of consciousness. Those who have no knowledge of God and their relationship to God may be forced out of their bodies by disease, accident, or old age; but those with a right understanding of God will make the transition without struggle, pain, or infirmity. All eventually will leave this plane.

"In my Father's house are many mansions." We pass from infancy to childhood, childhood to adolescence, and adolescence to maturity—each state of consciousness, one of God's many mansions. Those who accept the transition from one state of consciousness to another as an activity of God, not looking back in a vain attempt to cling to states of consciousness which should have been outgrown, do not experience the infirmities of old age. Resisting the advancing years, as if they were something to be feared, produces many of the discords associated with age. Accepting the normal, natural change, which accompanies the transition from one stage of life to another, will enable us to look forward to the experience of the middle years and the advanced years with joy and confidence rather than with fear and dread.

There is no difference between the flow of God this minute or a hundred years from now. Actually, the life of God will never age or end. God has a spiritual work for each one of us and He has given us His ability with which to perform it. As long as there is work for us to do on what is called this plane of existence, God will maintain us in vitality, strength, youth, health, and wholeness. In such assurance, we no longer mistake longevity for immortality. Longevity is not immortality: it is merely a continuation of the present physical sense of existence. We are not concerned with the visible span of our years on earth, but rather with the demonstration of our eternal Selfhood, forever about the Father's business.

Every transition is for the glory of God and for the development of our individual Soul. Those of us who are approaching the middle years, and beyond the middle years, must learn to ask the Father, "What have you for me to do now?" Then, just as the flower blooms, fades, and then blooms again, so do old experiences give way to new. We pass through many transitional experiences, but death is never a part of any of these experiences.

Sooner or later, everyone on the spiritual path reaches the place in his development where he realizes that as one state of consciousness is exchanged for another in the progress from birth to death, so the experience of what is termed death is merely another transition in the ongoingness of life. Death is our interpretation of what we are witnessing; but those who have caught the first tiny glimpse of God understand that God is life eternal, life without beginning and without end, "for he is thy life, and the length of thy days." This vision can only come to those who have risen above the selfish desire to hold themselves and others in bondage to a familiar form. The worm must emerge from its cocoon in order to become a butterfly. Everyone and everything pass through transitional stages; but through spiritual evolution and development, each one ultimately finds himself sitting at the foot of the Throne of God, returned to the Father's House.

This does not mean the immortality of the Soul and the death of the body as it is usually understood. The body will die daily: the fingernails and hair are cut off and grow again; the skin sloughs off; the cells in the body are constantly changing; and yet despite these changes, the consciousness which is our true identity remains. Our training from infancy has instilled in us the idea that the body which we see in the mirror, or of which we are conscious, is I. We have identified the body as ourselves; whereas the body is an instrument for our use, just as an automobile is a vehicle which we use to transport us from one place to another. At no time are we identified with or as our automobile. We are always separate and apart from the automobile, but we utilize it as a means of locomotion. The automobile is no more "I" than the body is "I," because "I" is consciousness.

At some period or other in our experience, we must give up our concept of the body as constituting the sum total of our being and accept the truth of our spiritual identity as consciousness. There comes a time for us to cease living as human beings. This does not mean that we must die or pass on to obtain our spiritual estate. This is not the death of the body, but the transition taking place in consciousness, referred to by Paul as dying daily in order to be reborn of the Spirit. Every day we must consciously remove ourselves from the laws governing human experience and acknowledge the grace of God in the conscious realization that we are living in the Invisible, on the Invisible, and by the Invisible. In this reliance on the Invisible, we die daily, until one day we die completely and are reborn in Spirit. From that moment, life is lived on an entirely different level in which we are not subject to the laws of physicality but live under divine grace.

Transition is not primarily physical; it is an act of consciousness. The worm is transformed in the metamorphosis of the caterpillar into a butterfly. The caterpillar state of consciousness drops its worm-self and rises into its butterfly-self. Transformation takes place in consciousness and externalizes itself as form. As we begin to understand this new and startling idea, we will then perceive that this *I* which I am, is permanent and eternal:

In the beginning God: the nature of God, Consciousness, is a continuous state of eternal being; and God manifests Itself as you and as me. God maintains the continuity of Its own existence in Its infinite, individual form, forever and forever and forever. All those who existed in the beginning exist now, and those who exist now will exist forever.

The body is the temple of life. This temple is life itself formed, Spirit formed. Just as the brain is the avenue as which intelligence expresses, so is the body the avenue as which life manifests. Can life be separated from its temple? Life is the substance of which the body is formed; therefore, the body is as indestructible as life, and as ageless.

Within me is the spiritual life force, which is functioning from the within to the without. I do not have a life force; I am the life force. That life force constitutes my true being and flows into harmonious and infinite form. Consciousness is the law and the activity unto the body. Nothing can ever stop the being that I am, because I exist independently of what the world calls matter, confinement, or embodiment. The nature of my being is eternality.

The invisible activity of Truth, operating in my consciousness, is renewing me physically, mentally, morally, and financially. Day by day this inner Selfhood, which is my invisible being, is manufacturing whatever is necessary for the fulfillment of my earthly experience.

I may watch the body pass from infancy to youth, from youth to maturity, from maturity to middle cge, and from middle age to old age; but through every change of the body, I remain as an observer, "impenetrable, unentered, unassailed, unharmed, untouched." At nine, nineteen, or ninety, I shall be watching every change of the body, every change of expression. I will never leave me nor forsake me. I cannot leave me nor forsake me, because I is "me." I will always govern and protect me.

The only moment I can know is this minute. A minute ago has no existence; a minute from now will have no existence.

To me, the past, the present, and the future are now: it is this now in which I am living; it is now that I have always lived; and it is now that I shall always live. It is purposeless and pointless for me to look forward to a life one hundred or two hundred years from now. The only time I can live is now; and now, in this moment, God, the one Life, is expressing Itself. I do not express life: Life expresses Itself as my infinite, individual, indestructible being.

"Yea, though I walk through the valley of the shadow of death," Thou art there. Death is not annihilation; death is but a shadow that looks like death. Even through the valley of the shadow, I shall stand there watching myself pass through it, because I can never be separated from I: I can never die.

CHAPTER XIII

FEAR NOT

Fear thou not; for I am with thee: be not dismayed: for I am thy God: I will strengthen thee; yea, I will uphold thee with the right hand of my righteousness.   Isaiah 41:10

Fear not: "There remaineth . . . a rest to the people of God," a rest from anxious thought-taking, a rest from fear, a rest from doubt and concern. In this state of rest, the power of grace descends and the presence of God flows into immediate expression as our experience. Receive the gift of God without labor, struggle, or strain. In quietness and confidence, in a resting from anxiety and fear, let God reveal Itself. Let God express Itself. Let God live our lives. Let there be no more "I" or "you" separate and apart from the Father, but let the Father be our life.

In conscious union with God, the mind rests. The human mind is no longer concerned with the problems of today or tomorrow, because the Soul's union with God—the conscious realization of God—reveals God as the fulfillment of every need even before the need is apparent. Concern, fear, and doubt vanish in the midst of fulfillment; the true meaning of the words, "Fear not," is revealed. In conscious union with God, the mind of God functions as our mind, as our experience, and as our life. Then the human mind rests and performs its proper function as an avenue of awareness.

This state of rest is an inner peace which is not attained by anything in the realm of effect. Even a thought or a statement of truth is an effect, and that is why using the mind to repeat stereotyped statements about God often does not induce peace. It is not thoughts about God that result in answered prayer. Thought about God is not the creative principle of the universe: God, Itself, is the creative principle and God is known only when the human mind is at rest.

God is the consciousness of individual being; therefore, infinity is the measure of that being. Nothing can be added to you; nothing can be taken from you. No good can come to you; no evil can touch you: you embrace within your own being the infinity of good. "Son, thou art ever with me, and all that I have is thine." All that God is, is already established within you. You are that place in consciousness through which the infinite nature of God is revealing Itself. Therefore, good cannot flow to you: good expresses itself from within and pours out upon all who come within range of your conscious awareness of this truth. It is only necessary to refrain from taking thought, to relinquish all anxious, fearful thought—to be still.

"Be still and know; . . . in quietness and in confidence shall be your strength," your peace, permanence, and security—not in bomb shelters, not in bank accounts, but in Thy kingdom, in Thy peace. In that quietness and confidence there is rest, protection, care, co-operation. In quietness and in confidence, fear not. Fear not:

I am with you, and I will be with you even unto the end of the world. Drop your burdens at My feet; drop your burdens in the assurance that all good is embodied and embraced within your being. I will never leave you nor forsake you. If you make your bed in hell, I will be there with you.

If you walk through the valley of the shadow of death, I will
be with you—only walk in quietness, in confidence, and in
assurance; walk without seeking.

There is no peace; there is no rest for those who are seek-
ing outside their own being. The kingdom of God is within.
Accept My kingdom and be at peace. Accept My promise:
Now are you the sons of God. Now are you My heirs, joint
heirs with Christ, and all the heavenly riches are yours now
—now, not tomorrow; now, not yesterday. There is nothing
to be achieved tomorrow; there are no regrets for yesterday:
there is only this living now, this moment of rest in Me, *of*
confidence in Me.

All power is established within you. Do not look to man
whose breath is in his nostrils; do not put your faith or trust
in princes, no matter how high or how powerful. There is no
power external to you. Never fear any effect; never fear that
which is created: trust the Creator. Shall creation mean more
to you than the Creator? Shall you love that which has
been created more than you love the Creator? Can you fear
that which God has created? Is there a creator other than
God? Is there another creation, a creation apart from God?
"Lo, this only have I found, that God hath made man upright; but they have sought out many inventions." Do not
fear what man can think, say, or do. Do not fear the inventions or machinations of the human mind.

The thought of man is not power. "For my thoughts are
not your thoughts . . . saith the Lord." Never expect a blessing nor fear a curse from the thought of man. The evil that
men do rises no higher than themselves. All evil is self-destructive. It destroys only those who contrive it, but never
those toward whom it is directed. Evil is only a power to
those who give it power.

Anything that you accept as a power apart from God may
harm you, but of itself, it has no more power than a shadow
upon a wall. If you believe that another can injure you or

that you can injure another, then you will suffer, not from what someone else has done, or from what you have done, but from your belief that there is a power apart from your own consciousness. The harm comes, not from another, but from you, because of your deviation from truth. You must come out and be separate from the belief that good or evil can come to you.

Do not fear any evil thought or deed which is directed toward you or anyone else. Do not fear any person, and above all, do not resent or hate him, unless you would bind him to you by the loathsome chains of hatred. You must understand that evil can touch only that person who is entertaining it: therefore, never fear evil; never hate it; never resent it; but always respond with compassion.

Your good may be "evil spoken of"; it may even be considered weakness; but do not let that concern you. You have no responsibility for proving anything and you have nothing to prove. Let the world entertain its own concepts of God and man, of religion and of prayer. "Bless them that curse you, do good to them that hate you, and pray for them which despitefully use you and persecute you." Pray for their awakening, but never fear them and never resent them.

No good can *come* to you, because you are already established in good; no evil can disturb you, because God is the measure of your good. God is the infinity of your consciousness; God is the purity of your Soul. Nothing exists outside your own consciousness.

If there is no evil in your consciousness, there is no evil operating in your world. How can you determine whether or not evil is operating in your consciousness? Do you accept or recognize a presence or a power apart from God? If you do, then evil exists for you. Do you see something to hate, fear, or resent? Then you are seeing an image which you have created within yourself. Hatred, resentment, and fear are but figments of thought, the result of a self-created image, and are, therefore, without power, presence, or reality.

God is the fabric, the substance, and the law of your consciousness. Evil is but a suggestion or temptation to accept a creator apart from God. This suggestion you must handle within yourself, until you come to that place of rest in which the Word of God abides in you and you abide in this consciousness of truth.

Abide in the truth that God is the only power and you will discover that all blessings emanate from this truth maintained in your consciousness. Abide in the truth of God's kingdom established on earth. Abide in the truth that I am closer than breathing and nearer than hands and feet. Abide in the truth that your names are writ in heaven, that you are the Christed Son of God—the image and likeness of His divine Being, the manifestation of His glory. "I am come that they might have life, and that they might have it more abundantly."

Let your prayer be a resting from words, a resting from thoughts, a resting from desire. Take no anxious thought. The Spirit of Truth, the Comforter, will never leave you, even though every avenue or channel of good is closed. The Comforter is an activity of God within your own consciousness. As such it is as much an integral part of your being as is your own integrity, loyalty, or fidelity. The Comforter is within you; it is the "Peace, be still" to every storm without and to every disturbance within. Open the door of your consciousness and let the Comforter speak; let the Comforter be your assurance; let the Comforter be your supply, your health, the harmony of your home, and the peace of your inner life.

To live the spiritual life means to live in an atmosphere of absolute fearlessness, regardless of the circumstances. "Be strong and of a good courage, fear not, nor be afraid of them: for the Lord thy God, he it is that doth go with thee; he will not fail thee, nor forsake thee . . . it is I; be not afraid." This is the greatest healing truth ever revealed to human consciousness. To the disciples a storm threatened death and disaster, but the Master saw only another opportunity to reassure them with those comforting words, "It is I, be not afraid." This same confidence enabled Jesus to stand before Pilate and say, "Thou couldest have no power at all against me, except it were given thee from above." It was this same power in Joseph that said to the brethren, "It was not you that sent me hither, but God. . . . God did send me before you to preserve life."

The circumstances confronting you may appear terrifying and disaster imminent, but the Christ says, "It is I; be not afraid." God has strange ways of bringing you to Himself. Sometimes that which appears as disaster and the dissolution of that which you hold most precious is the very means of awakening you to the spiritual life.

Never look upon temporary discord as failure, lack of demonstration, or the absence of spiritual vision and understanding. It was not lack of spiritual vision which drove Moses and the Hebrews into the desert experience; it was God leading them to a higher sense of good. It was not lack of understanding that sent Elijah into the wilderness to be so an hungered that ravens had to bring him food: it was God proving to Elijah that there remained seven thousand who had not bowed their knees to Baal and that even in the wilderness, there am I with thee and able always to set a table before thee, in the presence of thine enemies.

It was not failure that took Jesus up into a high mountain, there to be tempted of the devil, or that brought him to the wilderness without food: it was God's way of revealing that he was not to seek demonstrations of things, that man does not live by bread alone but by every word that proceedeth out of the mouth of God. It was not failure that placed the Master on the cross, that incarcerated Peter and Silas in a prison cell, that fastened an asp on the hand of Paul. No, these were God's opportunities provided to prove the nothingness of that which the world called an evil power, even a deathly power.

Never look upon the discords and inharmonies of your life as if they represented a lack of understanding or a lack of demonstration. Regard these unfortuitous circumstances as opportunities which will be dissolved when they no longer serve their purpose as spurs to your spiritual unfoldment.

Have courage to look at every person and circumstance that you consider harmful or destructive. In the silence, face the situation fearlessly; face the condition or the person and you will discover that it—or he—is an image of your own thought; and, therefore, there is no cause, jurisdiction, or law to support it. Recognize God as the Soul of every person and God as the activity in every situation.

Fear not what mortal thought can think or do, since mortal thought is self-destructive. Fear not the thoughts or deeds of man whose breath is in his nostrils. You are the temple of God, and God is in His holy temple now. You are the temple of the living God; your body is the temple of the living God; your life, your soul, your mind is the abiding place of truth, and if you abide in this truth and let this truth abide in you, no evil will come nigh your dwelling place. Fear not; rest in faith and confidence in the kingdom of God.

I *will never leave thee nor forsake thee. Why all this struggle? I am in the very midst of thee, closer than breathing, nearer than hands and feet. Why struggle as if you had to seek for Me and search for Me? Why struggle as if you had to hold on to Me? I will never leave you; I am with you always.*

I *will give you water. I will give it to you, so do not struggle for it; do not strive—just be still. Let Me feed you. Do not try to live by bread, at least not by bread alone; live by every word, every promise of Scripture which is fulfilled in you. As I was with Moses, so I will be with you. Believe only, and I will give you of the hidden manna which is invisible to the world, incompatible with common sense, and incompre-*

hensible to human understanding, hidden in the depths of your own being. I have meat the world knows not of. If you ask Me, I will give you water. Leave your dependence and faith in people, circumstances, and conditions. Deep down within you, there is a meat that the world knows not of; there are hidden springs of water and hidden manna: all this is embedded and embodied within your own being.

Your heavenly Father knoweth that you have need of these things; it is His good pleasure to give them to you— not to make you struggle and strive for them, but to give them to you, through grace. Whenever an appearance of discord looms upon your horizon, relax, rest, be at peace in the assurance of My presence within you.

Listen to Me, the still small voice at the center of your being. I will never leave you; I will never forsake you. Even in the valley of the shadow of death, I will be with you. You will never know death; you will never die. I give you living waters that spring up into life everlasting. If you listen for My still voice, if you rest in the everlasting arms, if you relax in Me, if you let My every word feed you and be your bread of life and your staff, you will never die. My Spirit is with you; My presence goes before you; I go to prepare a place for you.

Stop fearing; stop doubting. Rest in My bosom; rest in My arms; rest in My love and be at peace. Trust the I at the center of your being. Believe that I can do these things. Believe that there is a Presence at the center of your being whose only function is to bless, to be a benediction, and to be the instrument of My grace. Trust Me; believe only in Me; fear not.

CHAPTER XIV

THE TABERNACLE OF GOD

How amiable are thy tabernacles, O Lord of hosts. . . . My soul longeth, yea, even fainteth for the courts of the Lord: my heart and my flesh crieth out for the living God. PSALMS 84:1-2

One thing have I desired of the Lord, that will I seek after; that I may dwell in the house of the Lord all the days of my life to behold the beauty of the Lord, and to enquire in his temple. PSALMS 27:4

Lord, who shall abide in thy tabernacle? who shall dwell in thy holy hill? . . . He that hath clean hands, and a pure heart. **PSALMS 15:1; 24:4**

People of every faith have had their holy place of worship —a temple, mosque, or church—where the earnest seeker could tabernacle with his God. The structure, itself, and the objects of devotion within the sanctuary were all designed to lead the Soul to God; but, in reality, meeting God face to face is not dependent upon worship in a particular place or upon adherence to a prescribed ritual. The rites practiced are but the outer symbols of an inner search for God, and each symbol has its own deep meaning and significance. An illustration of this search for God, and one replete with symbology, is the worship in the tabernacle of the Lord as described in minutest detail in the Old Testament.

The Hebrew temple or tabernacle was in the shape of a parallelogram, with its sides facing north and south, and its ends east and west. It consisted of three parts: the outer court; the holy place; and the Holy of Holies.

The court was open to all for worship. In this outer courtyard was found a burning brazier, which was a great brazen altar, located near the entrance, into which offerings, voluntarily brought by the people, were burned. Between the brazier and the door of the temple stood a laver, constructed of brass, where the priests of the temple washed their hands and feet, preparatory to offering sacrifices or before entering the temple.

The holy place was accessible only to the priests. On the north side of it stood a wooden table. This was the table of shewbread on which lay twelve loaves of unleavened bread divided into two separate piles. This bread was indicative of God's abundance and grace, and every week a fresh supply was laid upon the table. The word "shewbread" means "bread of the Presence" and is interpreted by some biblical scholars as being symbolic of the presence of God. On the opposite side of the temple, across from the table of shewbread, stood the golden candelabra, a metal shaft with three branches on each side bulging into almond-shaped bowls, which formed receptacles for seven lamps. In these lamps olive oil burned continuously. Near the entrance to the Holy of Holies, and similar in construction to the brazen altar in the courtyard, was a golden altar in which incense, consecrated for this purpose, was burned by the high priest both morning and evening.

The most sacred spot in the whole tabernacle was the Holy of Holies, located just beyond the holy place. In this enclosure symbols of the greatest value and significance to the ritual were deposited, and only once a year were the priests allowed to enter its sacred precincts. Here reposed the ark of the covenant, a chest of acacia wood, overlaid with gold. Here, it was believed, the very presence of God could be found; but only those with clean hands and a pure heart could find their way to this Presence.

Now, through meditation, let us attempt to understand the spiritual significance of the symbolism of this temple worship. We begin in the courtyard. At the brazen altar, which greeted all those who entered, the worshipers delivered up their sacrifice. In those early days, the sacrifice usually consisted of consigning to the flames some material object of intrinsic value, thereby proving the sincerity of one's devotion and the willingness to give up all in order to reach God. The seeker had to rid himself of whatever it was that acted as a barrier to his communion with God and be willing to throw into the burning fire all those things which would impede his progress. This practice symbolized the sacrifice of personal sense, because no one can approach the presence of God without first giving up his faith and trust in human dependencies.

Some of us may never enter a temple, church, or a holy place of any kind; but nevertheless, if we truly desire to reach God, there is a sacrifice which is required of all of us. And what is the sacrifice demanded of us in this modern world, if we are to reach the Holy of Holies? What is the barrier confronting us? What is obstructing our progress? Is it not above all the age-old practice of worshiping other gods, forgetting the first commandment, "Thou shalt have no other gods before me"?

The gods we worship today are not graven images as of old. No; instead, fame, fortune, and position are idolized. We are continually looking to someone or something for satisfaction, expecting love and gratitude from people rather than looking to God as the source; or we are believing that our supply is dependent upon investments, bank accounts, and employment. This dependence on human means—*this* is the sacrifice required of us, one which is not offered in public, but which is delivered up in the sanctity and secrecy of our own being.

We cannot come into the presence of God weighted down by our burdens. Even the desire to influence God to intercede in our human affairs must be abandoned. Remember, the ark of the covenant—God—is at the far end of the temple; but before God can be reached, every barrier must be removed. So we begin to make the sacrifice by figuratively casting into the burning brazier all worldly dependencies. We must give up our mortal and material sense of wealth and of health; and yet we do not renounce these. On the contrary, as these human concepts are relinquished in a complete dependence on God, they may be present in ever-increasing abundance and harmony.

Let us not misunderstand the nature of the sacrifice. We are not required to give away or to throw away our personal possessions; it is the belief that material wealth constitutes supply which must be sacrificed. Unless this belief is discarded, we cannot come into the realization of our self-completeness in God, in which supply is already established in us from everlasting to everlasting. Lack and limitation are experienced only in proportion to the acceptance of the materialistic concept that money is synonymous with supply or that money is the source of supply. The reverse is true: supply is the source of money; supply is the substance of which money is formed. Supply is the consciousness of truth, the consciousness of our relationship to God. Once this relationship, this awareness of true identity, becomes a reality and an integral part of our consciousness, never again will we suffer lack or limitation, because this understanding is the substance of our supply.

The same spiritual wisdom or understanding which forms the substance of our supply also is the substance of our health. The commonly accepted view of health is that of a heart beating normally, a liver secreting the proper amount of bile, lungs inhaling and exhaling rhythmically, a digestive tract assimilating and eliminating satisfactorily, and various other organs and parts of the body performing their natural functions. This concept, that healthy organs and functions constitute health, must be sacrificed. Health is the realization of God as the source of all activity and the substance of all form, of God as the law unto Its creation. This spiritual wisdom will appear *as* health.

The material concepts of health and of wealth are but two among many erroneous concepts which must be sacrificed. Let us begin where we are this moment in consciousness. In our innermost minds and hearts, we, ourselves, know what we are entertaining of a mortal, material, limited, or finite nature, whether it be of wealth, health, friends, family, social position, power, or fame. We give up our human concepts to accept in exchange a higher spiritual sense of being; we sacrifice the worthless to receive that which is divinely real. Those who have sought God for their own purpose have missed the way: God can be attained only by a complete surrender of every desire, except the desire to bask in His love and grace. In this meditation we begin to make the sacrifice:

I surrender; I surrender every material obstacle, every mortal and human obstacle, everything that stands between me and God. In Thy Presence is fullness of life. I surrender every desire that I have ever had. I surrender every desire but one: all that I seek is Thee. Let me be in Thy Presence. Thy grace is sufficient for me—not Thy grace and health or wealth, but Thy grace alone. I surrender the desire for person, place, thing, circumstance, or condition—even my hope of heaven. I surrender every desire for recognition, for reward, for gratitude, for love, for understanding. I am satisfied with Thy grace. If only I can sit here and hold Thy hand, I will never ask even for tomorrow's breakfast; I will fast the rest of my days. Just let me hold Thy hand and I shall never hunger; I shall never thirst. Only let me hold Thy hand; let me be in Thy Presence.

Having divested ourselves of human and material dependencies by throwing them into the burning brazier, we are ready for the next step. A short distance beyond the smoldering fire stands a large round receptacle filled with water. This is the laver or bath, where is performed the rite of purification. Here the worshiper was given the opportunity of cleansing himself externally as well as internally. The cleansing process at the laver, however, is no more a physical operation than was the throwing of our sacrifice into the fire. Now as we stand before the laver, this is our opportunity to cleanse ourselves within and without. No one needs to be told about the things in his own mind of which he would like to be purified, because each person knows his own inner being better than does anyone else. The entire procedure resolves itself into a symbolic internal and external cleansing, in which occurs a complete purification of our human sense of good.

The sacrifice and purification of a human sense of values prepares us for entrance to the holy place. There we stand before the table of shewbread, which is always maintained fresh and abundant, not for the purpose of feasting, but as an evidence of the omnipresence of supply and of all good. In the contemplation of this table, there arises within us a silent recognition, that just as this shewbread is always present in the holy temple, so the bread of life and all that represents self-completeness is here this moment. And where is here? Where I stand. Right where I stand is the shewbread. Right where I stand is the omnipresence of the substance of life, the staff of life, the harmony and the good—all this, the gift of God. This gift of God is omnipresent and infinite, because it is of God, the infinite substance of all life.

Sacrifice, purification, and the contemplation of the abundance of good serve as a preparation for the opening of consciousness to the ever-abiding presence of spiritual light, which is represented by the seven-branched candelabra, located on the left-hand side of the holy place. The priests of the temple used seven lamps, because seven expresses completeness. As we stand in the presence of this symbol of spiritual light, the unextinguishable light of the Christ begins to permeate consciousness. **Now this seven-ness, this com**pleteness of spiritual illumination, infuses our being; and gradually or suddenly, consciousness awakens to the truth that right where we are now in meditation is the omnipresence, the allness of spiritual wisdom, spiritual understanding, and spiritual life. Whether or not the manifestation of this spiritual completeness is visible is unimportant. The full light of God, the full spiritual illumination, is complete within us now, even though it may not be apparent. Standing in meditation before this seven-lighted candelabra, filling ourselves with the remembrance of our self-completeness in God and believing that it already *is*, we let this light pour forth into visible expression.

Step by step, we are making our way to the Holy of Holies, the very presence of God. Each act of consecration brings us closer to our goal. Only one thing more is required—a final proof of devotion. So we turn in thanksgiving to the place of worship, symbolized by the incense burner, and there offer up our praise and gratitude for the innumerable blessings of God. Here, in this hallowed place before the burning incense in front of the sanctuary, we bring to conscious remembrance our progress since entering the courtyard. All that we have found so far in the temple has been a revelation of that which is already established within our own being. For none of this are we seeking or praying. Our self-completeness in God *is*, and for this we give praise, thanksgiving, devotion, worship, and adoration.

Each rite of consecration plays its own peculiar role in our spiritual unfoldment—the inner sacrifice thrown into the burning brazier, the purification of self at the laver, the contemplation of God's goodness before the table of shewbread, the recognition of the eternal light within symbolized by the lighted candlestick, and the offering of thanksgiving and praise at the golden altar. If each one of these rites has been performed faithfully, we stand directly behind the altar of incense, before a mistlike veil, which is finally withdrawn revealing the ark of the covenant.

If our meditation has been gentle and serene, bringing us into such a realization of our God-being, that our eyes are opened to spiritual reality, we shall behold the great mystery: the mist disperses; the curtain is withdrawn; and we find ourselves in the presence of God. There is no more mental or spiritual darkness. The presence of God announces Itself, reminding us:

I *am ever with you. I was with you when you began your search, but the mist before your eyes so dimmed your vision that you could not see* Me. *You were so cluttered up with materialistic concepts that your awareness was dulled. The mist could not be dispelled until those things which caused the mist had been removed. Then, and then only, could you find* Me, *hear My voice, and feel My Presence.*

In whatever state or stage of consciousness the seeker, whether priest or neophyte, finds himself, there is a Way for him—a Way which will lead him ultimately to the very presence of God. This Way may be completely unique to the individual or it may take one of the established forms of religious worship, such as: journeying from the outer courtyard to the very Holy of Holies in the Hebrew temple; placing a flower before a statue of the Buddha; making a pilgrimage to Mecca; bathing in the sacred Ganges; pondering the enigmatic *koan*; or kneeling in the cathedral in holy communion, drinking the symbolic wine, and eating the sacred bread.

Whatever symbology is used, it is dead and fruitless until the inner meaning of the form is discerned. Meditation such as this in which we have just engaged, clothes the symbol with life and reality. The act of sacrifice, purification, and devotion must be performed by each and every aspirant, not as a ceremonial demanded by some outer rule, but as the dictate of the heart. Only when the heart has yielded and the Soul has paid homage to God can we come into the Presence.

No one can enter the Presence except in holiness. Of old, only the priests were considered sufficiently worthy to gain admittance to the Holy of Holies; but today in our enlightenment, any spiritualized man or woman who has an understanding of his true identity is a priest and can find the Way to the inner sanctuary. Everyone who attains some measure of awareness of God is a priest. Such a person not only serves God, but is maintained by God. The divine bread of life feeds him; the invisible robe supplies him; and the light of truth illumines him, making him the light of the world, the avenue through which spiritual wisdom, love, life, and truth flow to all those who do not know the source of their good.

Thou wilt shew me the path of life: in thy presence is fullness of joy; at thy right hand there are pleasures for evermore.
PSALMS 16:11

CHAPTER XV

THE BEAUTY OF HOLINESS

Give unto the Lord the glory due unto his name:
O worship the Lord in the beauty of holiness.

PSALMS 96:8, 9

Behold, the heaven and the heaven of heavens is the Lord's thy God, the earth also, with all that therein is.

DEUTERONOMY 10:14

The heavens declare the glory of God; and the firmament sheweth his handywork.   PSALMS 19:1

Meditation is not an end in itself. That which we are seeking is a conscious realization of the presence of God, but in the realization of that Presence, before the experience of the full and complete illumination, there may be two of us—God and me. We do not want God *and me*: we want *God alone*. That is the final step on the spiritual Path.

God is unknown and unknowable to the human senses. One way, however, in which to bridge the immeasurable span between materiality and spirituality is to let thought drift from the cares and problems of the world to God's handiwork. In everyone's surroundings, there is always some object of beauty: a picture, a piece of sculpture, a plant, lake, mountain, or tree. We think of some one of these in meditation, considering the idea of God, the Invisible, expressing Itself through nature or through the mind of an artist or craftsman.

The presence and the power of the Invisible is that which is made manifest to us as the visible, the one inseparable from the other. Even a little understanding of God enables us to discern, in a measure, God's life, love, and joy embodied in man and the universe. In this understanding, our life and love expand and become more pure, joyous, and free, leading us into a higher dimension of life. We begin to live not so much in the world of effect as in the world of cause, discovering our good in the Cause of all that exists rather than in effect—in things, persons, or places. The more understanding we have of Cause, God, the greater is our enjoyment of all persons and things.

Only through penetrating the realm of the Invisible, this higher or fourth dimension of life, do we begin to perceive the law of love at work. To enter the fourth dimension, which cannot be comprehended by means of the physical senses, we visualize the invisible forces of nature which operated to bring into manifestation such a form as a plant or flower. With the eyes partially closed, look at a plant; look at its leaves, its buds, its flowers. What miracle of invisible activity has transformed a dry seed, a handful of earth, and a little water into a flower! The invisible life, operating through the moisture in the ground, touched the seed, broke it open, and caused little shoots to take root. This same invisible force drew from the elements of the earth the sustenance necessary to develop these shoots into a root system, which finally appeared above the ground as a plant. What marvel, what wonder, what miracle is this unfolding before our very eyes, unseen, unknown, inexplicable! Only God, the Infinite Invisible, could produce such beauty and grace.

All that appears is the form and activity of that which is invisible; the visible is but the appearing in form of that which caused it and gave it life and beauty. Because the form is inseparable and indivisible from its source, even the form is eternal. To recognize and understand the source of the outer symbols of creation is to love and enjoy them more keenly. The activity of nature is not something separate and apart from the plant. The invisible life of the plant takes form as its color, grace, and beauty.

In like manner, the soul, the mind, and the skill of an artist coalesce in a piece of stone or ivory to form a work of art in which the qualities of the artist are inseparable from the figure created. On the table before us is a tiny ivory representation of the Buddha. Let us try to visualize the artist seated before the piece of ivory, which he has painstakingly selected for its beauty and purity of color. Can you imagine how lovingly he fondled this inert mass as its ultimate form began to take shape in his mind? Can you see beyond the man, himself, and discern the beauty of soul, the purity of mind, the divine intelligence which guided and gave skill to his fingers? Remember, he was not merely carving the figure of a man: the Buddha represents enlightenment, a state of divine consciousness, that which the Occident calls the Spirit of God in man, the Christ, or spiritual Son. In the artist's mind is the desire to share with others his conception of this Spirit of God in man. Understanding the sculptor's love for his work arouses in us a deeper appreciation of the subject and the artistry expressed in this figure.

Just as the artist has poured himself out as this little figure or as nature has poured itself out as a beautiful flower; so do we live by the grace of an invisible Presence and Power, which is forever pouring Itself out as creation. In this form of meditation, we not only delight in beautiful sunsets, towering mountains, or starry skies; but seeing them, we see beyond them to the love, the skill, and the integrity of the Invisible, manifest as God's handiwork. The ceaseless activity of divine Love guarantees the continuity of this magnificent creation called man and the universe.

Meditation on the activity of God appearing as natural

phenomena or as any other form of beauty will teach us to look through man to his divine origin, taking no cognizance of his failures or successes. God has expressed Itself, Its own qualities, as every man, woman, and child. All the forces of the Invisible unite to form the visible expression of intelligence, life love, and joy. This is not discernible through a cursory observation of a person, any more than is the invisible cause of a plant or work of art perceptible to the senses. Only by looking through the appearance to the Invisible is Its essence discerned.

In the light of such perception, every individual is recognized as an expression of the infinite divine Being pouring Itself into manifestation. Criticism and condemnation are transformed into a deep love for this universe and its people. With this transformation will come compassion for those who know not their true identity, for those whom we have considered the evil men and women of the world.

Only in the degree that we understand the nature of God can we understand the nature of individual being. In thinking of ourselves, as well as of others, we must catch some glimpse inwardly of the nature and activity of God, the creative Principle, which brought us forth into expression. God has incarnated Itself as the very mind, soul, substance, and life of our being—even the substance of our body. The Word has become flesh as individual you and me.

Meditation must always have God as its subject and God as its object, because subject and object are one, not two. It should carry us from our three-dimensional life, the visible, to the Invisible, which is known as the fourth dimension. Those who live in a three-dimensional world live only in the world of height, width, and depth; in other words, they live in a world of form, completely separated from the essence of that which appears outwardly as the form. In the fourth dimension, in which God is the cause, substance, and the reality of life, all effect, whether appearing as thing or man, is revealed as but the showing forth of the infinite Being, God.

All individual being, all individual form, whether animal, vegetable, or mineral, is the invisible God, pouring Itself into expression, embodying Its infinite qualities, nature, and character. All of this earth is the Lord's and the fullness thereof: God appearing as a universe and as man. All of it is immortal; all of it is eternal; all of it is ours. "Son, all that I have is thine," and I am ever with thee. "I and my Father are one." How can we be separated from God? "Thou seest me, thou seest the Father that sent me." Can the love of the artist ever be separated and apart from that which it has created? We see the ivory figure; we see the state of consciousness that evolved it. How can the greatness or grandeur of the invisible life force of nature ever be separate from its form? We see the plant, we see the divine life force which formed it—they are one, inseparable, and indivisible. In the fourth-dimensional world, cause and effect, subject and object are one.

Gradually we go deeper and deeper until we find ourselves centered in God. We are not thinking any more: thoughts are being thought *for* us, ideas are being crystallized *through* us, impartations of the Soul become apparent to our awareness. Then we find God revealing Itself, uttering the Word, which is quick and sharp and more powerful than a two-edged sword: that Word of God which separates the Red Sea when necessary, which produces the cloud by day and the pillar of fire by night—the miracles in our experience. This meditation is a revelation of the Infinite Invisible declaring Itself within our own being.

Meditation is the art of divine appreciation, through which we learn rightly to appraise man, his achievements, and the universe. Our appreciation of the outer forms is increased, because meditation gives us an understanding of the divine Love which produced the form. When we understand the mind and the soul that has produced any form of good, we can better appreciate the good itself. To know the author of a book makes the book more meaningful; to know the composer of a piece of music makes the music more en-

joyable. If we could only know God, if we could only taste
or touch one drop of God, creation would appear in all its
wonder and glory. Meditation develops the insight which
carries us from the object to its creative principle, and then,
with this new insight, the world is revealed as it really is.

Through meditation, a new dimension of life will unfold.
No longer will we be limited to time or space, to height,
width, or depth, because instantly the mind will leap from
the three-dimensional form to the fourth dimension, which
is its origin, cause, and source. In this higher dimension, we
are not dependent on things which do appear, whether it is
person, place, or thing: we do not love them too much,
hate them, or fear them, because if we look through them, we
perceive, in every instance, that the source is God.

When we hear the words "I will never leave you nor
forsake you," let us remember the little ivory figure. The love,
the artistry, the skill, and the devotion of the artist can never
be removed from that figure. So it is with us. That which
formed us will never leave us nor forsake us. Its essence is
our very being.

Meditation on God's handiwork is one way of bringing the
Soul-faculties into active expression and of understanding
the higher wisdom. We must learn to look not only at sunsets, gardens, or any beautiful appearance, but to look beyond
them and catch a glimpse of that which brought them into
expression. Then we shall always have permanent forms of
beauty and permanent forms of harmony, because we shall
have that perfect divine Essence which is ever forming Itself
anew. If we try to see perfection in the form, we lose it. Material sense sees the form and enjoys it; spiritual sense sees
the underlying substance and reality of the form. The form,
then, is always perfect, complete, and whole.

The object of our work is to elevate ourselves to that
divine apprehension where we see God appearing in all of
God's glory—not in man's glory, but God's glory as the glory
of man—showing forth the infinite perfection of God's handi-

work. We are lifted into a state of divine illumination in which we behold God's world already perfect and complete, God manifesting Itself in all Its glory. "The heavens declare the glory of God," and the earth showeth forth His handiwork. And now "my meditation of him is sweet, and I am **glad in the Lord.**"

PART THREE

MEDITATION:

THE FRUITS

CHAPTER XVI

THE FRUIT OF THE SPIRIT

In the life of every seeker after God there comes a time when he feels the Presence and becomes aware, in one way or another, of an actual transcendental Presence and Power. Then he will have done with reading books about the God-experience or with hearing people talk about it. We do not know in what form that experience will come to us. To each one it comes in a different way, but this much is certain: When it comes, and the Spirit of the Lord is a realized Presence, "there is liberty"—a liberty and a freedom from the thoughts and things of this world, its fears, doubts, cares, and problems. The very moment that the Spirit of the Lord touches a person, he is transformed. He begins to understand the meaning of rebirth or of being "born again." He senses a difference within himself and he knows that he is not the same person he was yesterday or last week. The degree of the transformation may not at once be apparent in the **visible realm, but, bit by bit,** it becomes evident to the outer world.

Sometimes in the very beginning it may become evident in negative appearances. Loss often precedes gain: "He that findeth his life, shall lose it: and he that loseth his life for my sake, shall find it." The present sense of life must be sacrificed that the spiritual sense of life may be gained. Before the full and complete realization of this new life has taken place, the breaking up of the old forms may appear as a problem of some sort, either economic, emotional, or physical. There is the sense of losing something, giving up or sacrificing something. Actually, this is not true. Once the Spirit of the Lord has really touched a person, he is not disturbed or affected by outer appearances, because he recognizes them as part of a transitional experience.

The early Christian martyrs who turned from the pagan gods to the one God did not think in terms of a human sense of life. The persecution they were forced to endure was as nothing in comparison with the fulfillment of their spiritual mission. To the onlooker, it did not make sense that righteous men should be stoned, thrown to the lions, or burned at the stake. From the human point of view this never will make sense; but when the Spirit of the Lord has touched one, he understands that in reality nothing is being given up, lost, or sacrificed. It is martyrdom only to those who do not understand. To the spiritually illumined, it is the fulfillment of their spiritual destiny and experience, and that which is gained more than compensates for that which the world considers lost.

Today, the attitude of the man of the world is similar to that of the pagans of nineteen centuries ago. He views with amazement and distrust anyone who deliberately chooses to devote his time and money to the development of his spiritual nature rather than to the pursuit of pleasure, fame, and fortune—the gods of this world. Such a choice, in the eyes of the materialist, parallels the sacrifice of the Christian martyrs; but to a person who has even glimpsed the nature of the spiritual path, and more especially, to one who has experienced the Christ, what is gained more than compensates for that which has been given up.

In this life it is all highlands and lowlands—all mountains and valleys. Some days we look out on the world from the top of a pretty little hill, and all the world is gentle and kind; but before we know it, we have slid down into the valley. There are other days when we are way up on top of the highest mountain, only to find ourselves the following day giving way to discouragement and despair. These periods have no particular significance and are of no real importance; they are part of the rhythmic cycle of human life. The valley experiences are but a preparation for the mountain experience. There is always a valley between two mountains; one cannot ascend the next mountain without first passing through the valley lying between. In biblical terms, no man can find his life until he loses it. It is in the valley that he casts off the burden of the human self with its desires, wants, and wishes. Thus unencumbered, he is free to climb the next higher mountain. As the journey continues, the mountain experiences will be of longer duration and the valley experiences shorter. This will go on year after year, until a point of transition is reached when the heights remain his permanent dwelling place.

Today can be that day of transition for us. If we remember this day as the time when we made the decision to forget "those things which are behind, and [to reach] for those things which are before, [to] press toward the mark for the prize of the high calling of God in Christ Jesus," a year from now we shall have to admit that a transformation of our life is in progress. The human sense of life will never again touch us so deeply: we shall never again be able to hate or to love quite so intensely as before; we shall neither grieve nor rejoice with the same intensity of human emotion. The depth of our vision will continue to bring forth greater and greater spiritual light, wisdom, and guidance, so that every day will be a day of deeper discernment, a day of greater living in the atmosphere of God than the preceding day. This work will serve as a foundation on which we may build the temple of our body and home, the temple of our individual experience—a temple not made with hands, eternal in the heavens.

In this work we are at that place in consciousness where the Christ must be experienced. For years we have talked and heard about the beauty of the Christ, the power of the Christ, and the healing influence of the Christ—that Spirit of the Lord within us. Many of us also have been blessed through some other person's attainment of this Spirit of God. Now the time has come when we should no longer depend upon talk or upon the illumination of some other person. We must have the experience for ourselves, so that we can be in this world but not of it, walk up and down this world and yet not be a part of it, walk in and out of the discords and inharmonies, as well as the pleasures and harmonies of this world, and through it all maintain our spiritual integrity. We lose all sense of having to *do* something, or having to *know* something, or having to *understand* something. There is a relaxing of personal responsibility, and we rest in stillness and in quietness in the realization that where the Spirit of the Lord is, there is liberty. Let us be beholders, watching God at work in His universe, recognizing a transcendental Being as It performs Its work through our consciousness.

Some people have had an experience of God, but no outer transformation resulted. They have merely lived in the memory of it, because they did not know what it meant, how it had been attained, or how to maintain it. However, a student who has devoted his life to the study of spiritual wisdom and the practice of meditation finds that when the God-experience does come, he is not bewildered, because he understands its meaning. Although he accepts it with joy as an evidence of grace, he knows that it has been attained by the expenditure of much time and effort. Therefore, he does not live in outworn memories, because as receptivity increases through continued meditation, the God-experience will become more frequent, until the day comes when it can be attained at will.

This spiritual Presence and Power, this Christ, which takes over the functions of life for us, is invisible, but none the less real for all Its invisibility. It takes over the functions of the body, so that it becomes unnecessary to take thought for bodily activities. The Spirit within, the Christ, performeth that which is given us or our body to do. Gradually, as the Christ lives our life, the awareness of a physical body or of bodily activities as such is eliminated. Were it necessary to take thought to direct the circulation of the blood or the digestive tract, we would then be living by human means rather than by every word that proceedeth out of the mouth of God. No, the functioning of the body, without the need or help of any thought-taking, in fact, without any concrete knowledge of the operation of a blood stream or digestive system, is a direct evidence of Christ in action.

Health is of God, and in that recognition there is not my health or your health. If we accept this literally, we shall see miracles happen. Good is not personal, whether it is health or wealth. Health is really a quality and an activity of God, the essence and substance of God. To speak of "my" health and "your" health would indicate that there are degrees of health, good health and bad health. In the spiritual way of life this cannot be; it is an utter impossibility: there is only one health and that is God.

With God as health—and God "is the health of my countenance"—health is infinite, not because it is our health, but because it is God's health. Once we learn to give up the sense of personal possession as indicated by the words "I," "me," "mine," we begin to find the real meaning of spiritual living—universal, impersonal, harmonious living. God expresses Its harmony through our being. Every phase of harmony, whether it is goodness or good health, is a quality, an activity, and a law of God. When we recognize God as the essence of all good, we become instruments for the expression of a universal sense of good.

With the spiritual sense of health comes the discovery

that health is not dependent on digestion, on elimination, or on the functioning of any organ of the body. Health is dependent on God alone; it is a quality and an activity of God. Whatever is necessary in the government of the body is performed as an activity of God. Let us remember this in connection with the very food we eat: "The food that I eat has no nourishing value, no substance, no power to sustain **or maintain life; but I,** the Soul of me, the consciousness of me, impart to it, its substance, its value, and its nourishment." If we make that a conscious realization, we shall find that food will have an entirely different effect upon our bodies than it has had heretofore. "He performeth that which is given me to do," and, therefore, the activity of the body is performed by that *He* that is within us. We do not have to take thought about it. He performeth it. He perfecteth that which concerneth us. Let us be beholders of God appearing as our health, our wealth, our strength, and our life.

So it is with every phase of our human experience. If there is a sense of rightness about life—if the right words are spoken at the right time, if the right acts are performed at the right time, if harmony prevails in our experience—then, we feel, we see, we recognize that every phase of that experience is a direct result of the activity of the Christ. We do not do it; we do not take thought: It, the Christ, does it all, even before we have any awareness of what is transpiring. It, the Christ, is the activity of the body, of the purse, and of our relationships with one another. The Presence goes before us to make the crooked places straight and to prepare a place for us. The Presence does everything for us, and we live on this plane of existence as witnesses—beholders.

There are innumerable biblical passages which reveal the importance of "waiting on the Lord," of being a beholder of life. This does not mean sitting idly by doing nothing. On the contrary, the more one waits on the Lord, the more is one a beholder of God working in him, through him, and as him, and the more active does he become.

If we are beholders, we do those things which require our attention and which lie nearest at hand. If we have a household to take care of, we take care of it; if we are entrusted with a business to manage, we manage it; if we have calls to make, we make them; but while we are engaging in these activities, it is with the attitude: "I wait on the Lord; I behold what the Father gives me to do." Always we hold ourselves in such a state of receptivity that we are ready and willing, at a moment's notice, to change any plans we may have made in order to follow the divine plan.

There are duties to be performed and obligations to be met every day of our lives. That which is given us to do must be performed; but in being a beholder, we discover that there is a divine direction, a divine power which guides us. This is the state of consciousness achieved by Paul: "I live, yet not I, Christ liveth in me." It is as if the man Paul were stepping to one side saying: "The Christ is on the field; the Christ is acting in me, through me, and as me. Christ lives my life for me." That is the attitude that we maintain as a beholder, almost as if we were saying: "I am not really living my life at all. I am watching the Father live Its life through me."

This is the ideal way of living; this is the spiritual way of life, the way in which we meet with the fewest obstacles, the least opposition, the smallest number of misunderstandings. There is always a Presence, the Infinite Invisible, which goes before us to make the crooked places straight, and to make every detail of our experience perfect. It is only when "I" do things, say things, and think things that the outcome may be wrong. Our entire experience of frustration comes from our reluctance to wait long enough for It to take over.

Most of us are unwilling to wait until the moment in which a decision is necessary; we insist on knowing the answer in advance, the day before, the week before, or the month before. We want to know what is around the corner; we want to know today what is going to happen next week or next month, and even what decision should be made for next year, instead of waiting until the actual moment when the decision is required, and then letting God put the words in our mouth and reveal what action should be taken. Day by day the manna falls; day by day the wisdom, guidance, and direction necessary for that day are given to us. God does not often advise us a week in advance; we receive the direction as we need it. We have acquired the habit of impatience and the result is that instead of waiting for God's decision to be made manifest, we let fear creep in and then, afraid of the possibly unfortunate effects of indecision, rush in and act on the basis of our own best human judgment.

In spiritual living we do not depend upon our correct human evaluation of situations. Regardless of how good our judgment may seem to be, we turn from it to the Father: "Father, show me when to move; show me whether or not to take the next step and when to take it." With patience and with practice, we develop the consciousness of a beholder, of waiting on the Lord, which leads us to the miracle of life, in which we discover, not only that there is a God, but that It has become the governing factor in our life: It has taken over our experience. We have prevented the activity and operation of God in our affairs by not waiting, by not being a beholder, by not sitting, as it were, a little to one side of ourselves until we feel that the Father is taking over. If only we could do that, we would find the miracle of a divine Presence going before us to make all things new. When *we* make a decision, very often we find insurmountable obstacles in the way; but when *God* makes the decision, God goes before us and removes every obstacle. Everything necessary to facilitate the undertaking is provided.

Let us make a daily practice of being a beholder:

Father, this is Your day, the day You have made. I will be glad and rejoice in it. Reveal to me the work of this day; show me Thy decisions, not mine, but Thine. Let Thy will alone be the motivating and activating principle of my life.

Let us be willing to wait until the very second before a decision must be made; even if it is a minute later than necessary, we wait and wait. Let us be patient, very patient. It will come, and once we have had this experience, we shall have witnessed the miracle of watching God operating in our affairs. When this awaremenss has become an actual experience, we shall never again know what it is to be without a consciousness of God's government, because we shall have discovered that God does respond, that God does take over. In the 23rd Psalm we read that we are to dwell in the house of the Lord all the days of our life, *all* days: forever and forever I will dwell in this recognition of God's wisdom, and God's government. Once we have had the distinct feeling of being led by God, of Christ impelling us to act, we shall never again be satisfied to make a decision without recourse to spiritual guidance.

Many successful people testify to the importance of periods of quiet in which to draw on their inner resources for inspiration and direction. They have discovered that ordering their day, so as to permit short but frequent intervals of rest and relaxation from the cares of the world, releases them from a sense of pressure, refills their reservoirs, and they go forward with renewed vigor and interest. There is a limit to what the human mind and body can accomplish in twenty-four hours. The person on the spiritual path, however, who has learned to open himself to the activity of the Christ through meditation, knows no limitation. There is no limit to what *the Christ* can perform through a human being in twenty-four hours. The Christ does not measure Its activity in terms of individual capacity. It operates through Its capacity, for which we are but the instruments.

There is nothing which cannot be brought forth from the depths of our own inner being, because God is the mind of individual man. Everyone has the full capacity of the Godhead, and in proportion to the stillness and quietness of the thinking, reasoning mind does infinity flow through into expression. Both mind and body are instruments of God. Just as we use the arm and hand for writing, so does God use our minds and bodies for making Itself visible and tangible in human experience. As God reveals to us Its harmony, the mind and body serve as instruments to bring God's harmony into visible form and expression. Any inspiration received from God carries with it fulfillment. For example, if an inventor realizes that his work is the activity of God, all that is necessary for the fulfillment of the idea embodied in his invention will be available—the financing, the advertising, the buying, and the selling. This is true of any God-created idea. The source of its inspiration is the same activity which brings it to its full fruition.

Nobody could earnestly follow for any length of time the instruction in meditation as set forth in this book without noticing a change of a radical spiritual nature. From the moment that there is a turning away from material reliances to an invisible, humanly unknown way of life, it is inevitable that this change will follow. "The fruit of the Spirit is love, joy, peace, longsuffering, gentleness, goodness, faith, meekness, temperance: against such there is no law." Such fruit does not come to those who have not yet learned to value the Christ—Its presence, power, and jurisdiction. Years of consecration and devotion in which one has, in some measure, left all for Christ must precede the harvesting of this fruit. But when that time comes we shall never again be alone. We shall never again fear. We may go through the valley of the shadow of death, but even there the Presence is with us. We rest in the center of our being while the storms pass overhead. We are beholders of God, guiding, maintaining, and sustaining Its own, God fulfilling Itself as individual being. Then we "see Him as He is" and God appears as the wholeness, the abundance, the harmony, the peace, and the joy of our experience.

CHAPTER XVII

ILLUMINATION, COMMUNION,
AND UNION

Meditation leads to that illumination which becomes first, communion with God, and finally union. Illumination is an individual experience. In no way is it related to any outward observance or form of worship; it is entirely dependent upon the realization of our relationship to God. It is an experience which takes place within ourselves separate and apart from every other person. It cannot be shared with anybody—husband, wife, child, or trusted friend. It cannot be sought in the company of others. No two people can seek it together. Each must retire to the inner sanctuary of his own being and find his God-experience there. In a measure, it is possible to share our unfoldment with others who are either illumined or who are on the path of illumination, but let us always remember, a God-experience is an individual one. If it were to come to us in the midst of thousands of people, it would still remain a solitary experience. There can be no partner in this experience. We can share the unfolding truth which may lead others to the experience and, if we have a sufficient degree of enlightenment, we may help to lift them to the point where they also can experience God. Further than that we cannot go; the experience, itself, must take place within them.

No one should attempt to teach or share the truth which has been revealed to him, until he has let it work within his own consciousness and has, thereby, achieved a measure of light. After that he will be directed as to how, when, where, and under what circumstances he should share this revelation. God will make known the part he is to play and the way in which he is to play it.

Illumination is possible to every individual in proportion to the intensity of his desire for it; but while he is striving to make the God-contact, he would do well to keep that first spark hidden from the world, until it is kindled into a flame. After the first glimmerings of illumination, the wise student holds this new-born Christ close within his bosom, secret from the world. Figuratively, he goes down into Egypt to hide the Christ-Child. He does not speak of It; he does not in any way reveal It to the world, because the world, in its ignorance and thoughtlessness, may attempt to damage It. The world may uproot It, may even destroy his own confidence and assurance in Its presence and Its power. For this faith, the world would unhesitatingly crucify one. Always the world seeks to destroy the Christ. Prophecies, from the earliest scriptures known to man down through the ages, indicate that whenever the Messiah comes, he will be sacrificed. There is that in human nature which does not wish to be destroyed, and it knows that the one Power that can annihilate human wickedness, arrogance, and egotism is the presence and the power of the Christ realized.

It is necessary that we maintain secrecy. This is the one thing we dare not tell the world. The very moment the world senses in any person a pure devotion to the Christ, it would unhesitatingly speak evilly of him and attempt to tear him loose from his moorings. The Antichrist, or suggestion of a selfhood apart from God, enters with the subtlety of a serpent to arouse doubt and to undermine faith. It must be kept secret, therefore, until the time comes when the Christ-consciousness is so developed that It has become rooted and grounded in consciousness as the very activity of daily life. Then, we can stand before the world and reveal It and not be concerned or affected by any abuse or doubt the world may heap upon us. It is only when *we* are presenting the Christ to the world that we are in danger of losing It ourselves; when the Christ has taken over sufficiently, It presents *Itself* to the world silently, secretly, gently, and so quietly that no one in the world recognizes or knows what It is, but everyone feels Its influence.

After the first glimpse of illumination many temptations beset us. Even Jesus was faced with the temptation of lack, the temptation of fame, and the temptation of personal power. All these he resisted and overcame. These same temptations come to all of us, but any temptation that a human being has ever had is multiplied many times as soon as he obtains even a degree of spiritual illumination. As he goes on to greater illumination, however, these temptations fall away one by one until only one temptation remains —egotism, the temptation to believe that "I" of my own self can do something or be something. That, too, must finally yield to the risen Christ.

There is no limit to the depth of Christhood. Illumination leads to communion in which there is a reciprocal exchange, something flowing out from God into our consciousness and back again from our consciousness into the consciousness of God. It is meditation carried to a deeper degree than has been experienced thus far, but *we* do not carry it—*God* carries it. It cannot be brought about by any effort on our part; it cannot be forced. We can only be patient and wait for It and then find that It takes over and there is a peaceful, joyous interchange in which we feel the love of God touching us and our love for God returning to God.

In communion the activity of the Christ becomes a con-

tinuous experience—one realized not only at rare intervals
but ever present. Eventually, a transitional point is reached
in which a radical change takes place. We no longer live
our own life; Christ lives our life for us and through us;
we become nothing more nor less than an instrument for
this divine Activity: we have no will of our own; we have
no desire of our own; we go when and where we are sent;
we have no supply of our own; we do not even have health
of our own. God is living Its life as us. When God lives
our life, the robe of Spirit envelops us. Then, whenever
anyone touches our consciousness, He touches the robe of
the Christ, and if but the hem of the robe is touched,
there is healing and redemption. Enfolded in this robe, it
is unnecessary to go anywhere to carry the Christ-message
to the world; the world will reach out for It wherever we are
—but we must be robed with the consciousness of the
Christ.

Communion, carried to its ultimate, results in the final
relationship which is union with God. In communion, such
a high state of consciousness is reached that it is possible
to turn within at any time of the day or night and feel
the presence of the Lord. It is as if It were saying, "*I* am walking beside you"; then again It may say, "Heretofore, *I*
have walked beside you, but now *I* am within you"; finally,
you hear It say, "Heretofore, *I* have been within you, but
now *I am* you—*I* think as you; *I* speak as you; *I* act as you;
your consciousness and My Consciousness are one and the
same, because there is now only My Consciousness."

When that stage is reached, there is no longer communion,
because there are not *two*. There is on: one, and that one
is God expressing Itself, revealing Itself, fulfilling Itself. It
is the mystical marriage in which we witness ourselves being
wedded to the Christ—we become that which God hath
joined together in the indissoluble union which has existed
from the beginning. "I and the Father are one"—that is
the divine union. In this mystical union, every barrier is

dissolved, and even our intellectual opinions melt into the universal wisdom. There is a complete surrender of self into the universal One: All that I have is Yours, my hands are Yours, my very body. I have no need of any person, place, or thing; within me is the bread, the water, the wine. I have only fulfillment.

This is the height of spiritual experience. In the Song of Solomon this is the experience which is described almost as if it were a story of human love, but of course it is not that at all. Always there are at first the *two*. It is in the communion stage that it is the two who love each other—the Father and the Son. Jesus said, "As the Father hath loved me, so have I loved you." In this relationship of communion we feel our love flowing out to God and God's love flowing to us, as a mother's love enfolds her beloved child.

All this ends with union. When union takes place, there is no longer any "I." There is only God, and as we look out on the world, we see only what God sees; we feel only what God feels, because there is no other Selfhood. There is no you; there is no I; there is only God *being*.

These moments of union are priceless. They are few, but they are precious, because they reveal the world as it *is*. If it is possible to experience this union for a few days or even for an hour, it is possible to experience it forever. There is only one necessity: getting ourselves out of the way. The day will come when the earth will be so full of the presence of the Lord that there will be no mortal or material sense of existence left. Illumination will have dissolved every shadow cast by the individual who has thrust himself between the sun and its beam of light.

When illumination comes, we no longer need anything found in the outer world. Everything and everyone become part of our being. Never again is it necessary to take thought, because now God lives our life. There is always the consciousness of a Presence; It sings within us over and over: *I* will never leave you nor forsake you. It lives our life and we become beholders of It, watching It unfold as our very experience. There is that within which draws to us all that is required for our fulfillment. In the silence of our consciousness the creative power of God comes forth. When we feel that answering response, we are not only one with God, we are one with every spiritual being in the universe. Wherever or whatever there is of good for us in the universe, finds its way to us.

It is the goodness of God which pours through us to the world. No longer do we of ourselves own anything. It takes from us all sense of personal possessions, personal acquisitiveness, personal powers, and in their place bestows upon us *Allness*, the abundance of God in its infinite fullness. The whole glory of God is revealed in and as our life: as the harmony of our relationships, as the abundance and satisfaction found in our affairs, as the radiance of our countenance, as the buoyancy and strength of our body, as the very garments with which we are clothed. All the joy and fulfillment which surge through our being is a silent testimony that *I* in the midst of thee am mighty.

CHAPTER XVIII

A CIRCLE OF CHRISTHOOD

Is it reasonable to expect that there can be a whole group of people in modern times so dedicated to the Christ-life that they will live by actual spiritual contact? Is it conceivable that a body of students or earnest aspirants on the spiritual path will evolve, who will seriously accept the hypothesis that they, of themselves, are nothing, but that God is all? Is it within the range of possibility that a *group* of people will appear on this earth, who have arrived at that point of realization where life is lived by the Spirit? Such a group would establish a pattern for the whole world.

Always there have been isolated individuals who have achieved Christhood by grace, but at no period in the history of the world has it been either realized or maintained by a group. No one has been able to impart it to a group, because up to this moment no effective way of transmitting the Christ-consciousness to large numbers has been found—at least none that has been effective. It was imparted by Jesus to the twelve disciples, and out of the twelve only three or four were able to maintain it. It was taught to several students by Buddha, but only two of them understood it, and of Lao-tse's disciples, only one was able to carry on.

Today the wisdom of all ages is again coming to light in human consciousness: "Hear, O Israel: The Lord our God is one Lord." This teaching of oneness is the ancient secret of the mystics revealed throughout all time by every one of the great spiritual lights of the world. Every great religious teacher has caught this vision of oneness. This it is which enables us to unite in that selfsame realization that if I am in the Father, and the Father is in me, then, you are in me, and I am in you; and we are all one in the Father, united in one consciousness.

Despite the diverse forms of religious worship and teaching prevalent today, men and women of whatever persuasion should be able to unite in this age-old wisdom of oneness. The teaching of oneness is universal and in no way interferes with the continued practice of our present manner of worship. In reality, there is no cleavage between "your" teaching and "my" teaching. There is one Spirit and that Spirit is God, permeating human consciousness wherever human consciousness is receptive. This Spirit of God works through me for your blessing and through you for my blessing, since we are one in Christ Jesus.

The world has made great strides forward in religious and metaphysical teachings since those early days of Jesus, Buddha, and Lao-tse; but too much of this teaching has remained mere speculation in the realm of the intellect. Somehow, somewhere, a group known by their fruits must come into active expression, a group who actually live the Christ life. They must keep their fingers on their lips, not talking truth, not teaching truth, but living truth, their every act a demonstration of the presence and power of God. As discord or inharmony flash across their horizon, they will resist the temptation to affirm truth, and instead, turn to that center where the Christ is enthroned and let It make the crooked places straight. *It*, not they, will be the blessing.

The answer, the solution to all problems, is the realized Christ; let us call It the Risen Christ. Christ buried in the tomb of the mind will not come forth and do wonders, but Christ risen in our consciousness, Christ raised up from the tomb through meditation and communion—that is the miracle worker of the ages. It may begin with us and express in the improvement of our health, supply, and environment. Then, as the Christ becomes active in our consciousness on behalf of those who are receptive to It, It will begin to be an influence in their experience. Thus, going from one to another, touching a few here, a few more there, eventually, it will encircle the globe.

Every person who has prepared himself for the awakening of the Christ may become an integral part of this circle of light. It is not, however, an experience that is possible to every person at this present moment, just as it is not possible for everyone to earn a degree in engineering or law, without the required preliminary study. Much as all those who are interested in the deep things of the Spirit would like to include their friends and families as their companions along the Way, this is not always practicable. Often the members of one's own family or others closely related by ties of friendship, love, or association are the very ones who are the most antagonistic to truth. They are the rocky or barren soil to which the Master referred. It is not for anyone to judge or to know who is ready for Soul unfoldment. That is something between every person and his God. Eventually, every knee must bend, and ultimately, all will come into their spiritual heritage.

Spiritual unfoldment must begin with one—always one. It has to begin in the consciousness of one person. That consciousness could just as well be yours; that consciousness could just as well be mine. It all depends upon the degree in which we come into the realization of the Christ. The **realized, risen Christ,** active in one person, becomes a potent force in the entire world. At any given moment there may be a receptive person in some hospital, in a prison cell, on a battlefield, in high political office or low, someone anywhere in the world crying out, "O God, can you help me? Is there a God to help me?" Wherever or whenever there is a reaching out to God, there the realized Christ is, in Its fullness. No one can fully apprehend the widespread effect of the realized Christ when It is loosed in the world. There is no way of knowing how many people have had healings—mental, physical, moral, and financial—by the very act of reaching out to the Unknown, and, thereby, touching this very Christ, which has been released in meditation by you or by me.

It is for this reason that I have been asking our students in The Infinite Way to devote one meditation period each day to God alone—not for themselves, their families, their business, their patients, or their students, but for God alone. In other words, we reserve one period for a meditation in which we go to God with clean hands:

Father, I seek nothing. I come to You in the same spirit in which I would go to my mother were my mother available, for communion, just for love. You are the Father and Mother of my being. You are the Source of my life. You are the Soul of me, the Spirit of me. I have no favors to ask of You. I come to You for the joy of communion, to feel the assurance of Your hand in mine, the touch of Your finger on my shoulder—just to be in Thy Presence.

The realized, demonstrated presence of God is the Saviour of the world.

The time has passed for any one individual to set himself up as the sole representative of the Spirit of God on earth. Every person must show forth that same Spirit. If this book can bring to a few the experience of the Spirit of the Lord, then they, in turn, will be able to go out and help others reach this same experience. The Saviour is the Spirit of the Lord—not a man or a woman. The Saviour is the Spirit of the Lord, and the Spirit of the Lord must be realized by you and by me individually.

The most that any spiritual teaching or book can accomplish is to lead the student to the realization that there is a kingdom of God within him and then inspire him with the desire to achieve it. The most that a spiritual teacher can do is to open the consciousness of those individuals who look to him, so that they may attain the realization of the Spirit of the Lord. But one teacher, as we have seen in the case of Jesus Christ, could not do this for the entire world—not even for his own disciples, except for the few who were receptive and responsive. Judas is an example of one who did not respond to the Christ. Only those with a deep spiritual hunger can be lifted by a spiritual teacher into the God-experience.

Every mystic throughout the ages has succeeded in opening the consciousness of students to the experience of the Spirit of the Lord. In some cases, hundreds received it through their teacher. But the world went on its merry way to destruction, because those who reached this high state of consciousness set up a worship of the teacher rather than a practice of the teaching. Everyone who through this work is touched by the Christ should dedicate himself to opening the consciousness of others in the same way as has been done for him. This he can do by being a witness to the activity of the Christ in his own consciousness, demonstrating to the world that anyone with sufficient interest and devotion may be led to the same experience.

Wherever there is a realized God-consciousness, it becomes an instrument through which God functions in human consciousness. The activity of the Christ can function through my consciousness, reaching and touching yours to illumine, heal, and supply. In the same manner, as you are attuned to the Infinite Invisible in meditation, Christ finds an outlet through your consciousness, touching the lives of others, awakening their consciousness, and bringing what the world calls healing to their bodies and affairs. The activity of the Christ, with no human intervention, flows into whatever human consciousness is opening itself to God's grace.

The day will come when there will be a band, a circle of spiritual wisdom around the entire globe. The fabric of this circle will be formed throughout the world by the realized Christ-consciousness of teachers and students. When this circle has been developed sufficiently, then everybody who seeks spiritual light will be able to reach out and touch the realized Christ-consciousness of anyone in this band of illumined Souls. Then the world will be uplifted, not one by one, but by the millions. When this consciousness is released through individual realization in meditation and communion, it can no longer be localized in either time or space and anyone in the world who touches it can attain it in some measu͞.

Illumination dissolves all material ties and binds men together with the golden chains of spiritual understanding; it acknowledges only the leadership of the Christ; it has no ritual or rule but the divine, impersonal universal Love; no other worship than the inner Flame that is ever lit at the shrine of Spirit. This union is the free state of spiritual brotherhood. The only restraint is the discipline of Soul, therefore we know liberty without license; we are a united universe without physical limits; a divine service to God without ceremony or creed. The illumined walk without fear—by Grace.*

* From the author's *The Infinite Way* (San Gabriel, Calif.: Willing Publishing Company, 1956), p. 40.